Table of Contents

Using Games to Practice Skills

Students are always eager to play games. During this play much learning takes place. While an identified skill such as naming the letters of the alphabet is practiced, students are also becoming better listeners and observers and are taking turns and cooperating in a group.

"Playing" with a small group gives a teacher the opportunity to closely observe students, to see their strengths, and assess where they need more help. It is also easier to provide immediate positive responses.

When to Use

Play a game whenever you have a group of students needing to practice one of the skills covered in the games (see the table of contents for a skill list).

Many of the games in this book can be played in five- or ten-minute periods. Utilize aides, parent volunteers, and cross-age tutors to play games with small groups.

The games can also be sent home to be played with a parent or siblings.

How to Use

Select the games that are appropriate for your students.

Prepare the playing pieces in advance—this is a great time to call on parent volunteers. Many parents who are unable to come during school hours may be willing to make a game for class if you send materials and directions home.

Using Language Games in Centers

Most of the games and game variations in this book can be played by a pair of students. Many can be played as a sorting or matching puzzle by one student once they have played the game in the group.*

Follow these steps:

1. Make a copy of the playing pieces.
2. Color, cut out, and laminate the pieces.
3. Put the pieces in an envelope, a self-closing plastic bag, or an appropriately sized box with a lid.
4. Put a picture and the name of the game on the outside of the container.
5. Place the games on an accessible table or shelf.

Large games can be stored in a plastic or wire storage bin.
Small games can be stored in a shoe box or in the pockets of a hanging shoe bag or word card holder attached to a wall.

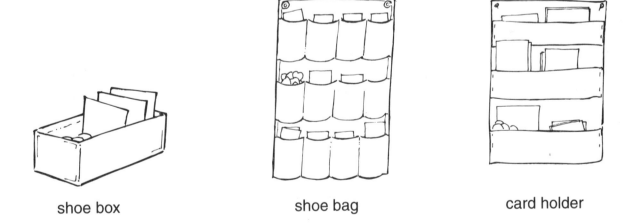

shoe box   shoe bag   card holder

*The following games don't work well in a center as they require adult interaction or several students to make them interesting.

Same or Different? (page 50)

5-in-a-Row (page 64)

What's Missing? (page 81)

The Three Bears (page 99)

Lollipops for Sale

How to Make

1. Use the pattern on page 6 to make a tagboard template. Trace the template on colored construction paper. You'll need two circles for each lollipop. Make one lollipop for each color you want to practice.

2. Laminate and cut out the circles.

3. Tape a tongue depressor on one of the circles as shown.

4. Glue the two circles together with the tongue depressor inside.

4

How to Play

1. Have students sit in a circle. Pick one student to be the lollipop seller.

2. The lollipop seller holds all the lollipops (or carries them in a can) and skips around the inside of the circle saying:

   > "I'm selling lollipops. I'm selling lollipops.
   >
   > I'm selling lollipops. Which one do you choose?"

   (Some young students aren't physically developed enough to skip. Have them walk around the circle.)

3. The seller stops on the word "choose." The student the seller stops in front of says:

   > "I'd like the ___(color word)___ lollipop, please."

4. The seller lets them take the lollipop to hold, and the seller continues skipping around the circle saying the verse. Play continues until all the lollipops are "sold."

   You may want to make a rule that if the seller ends up at someone who already has a lollipop, he/she moves to the next student so that everyone gets a turn.

5. Teacher collects the lollipops by asking for each one saying:

   > "Please bring me the ___(color word)___ lollipop."

6. If there is time, select a new seller and play again.

Playing with Beginners

The teacher holds the lollipops and walks around the circle saying:

> "I have a ___(color word)___ lollipop.
>
> I have a ___(color word)___ lollipop.
>
> I have a ___(color word)___ lollipop.
>
> The ___(color word)___ one is for you."

At "you" the teacher stops and gives the student she is standing in front of the lollipop. Continue until all of the lollipops are passed out. Then collect them as suggested in step five in the preceding activity.

Variation

Cut lollipops from white construction paper. Write a color word on each lollipop. Play the game as described above.

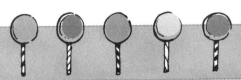

Pattern for Lollipops for Sale

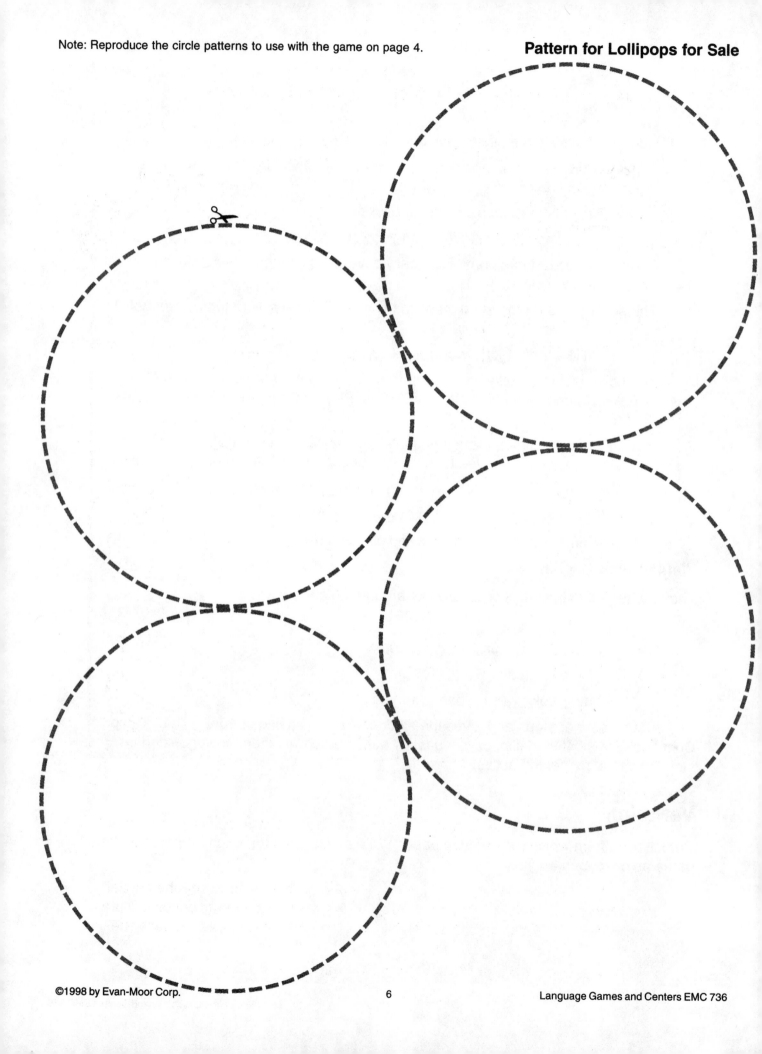

Follow the Footprints

How to Make

1. Reproduce the footprint patterns on page 10 on light brown construction paper or cut them out of tagboard. You will need one footprint for each letter you wish to practice.

2. Print the letters on the footprints. Younger students may need to see the capital and lower case letter together on the same footprint. As students become more skilled with the letter names put the capital and lower case letters on separate footprints.

3. Cut out the footprints.

How to Play

1. Tape the footprints in a line on the floor. Be sure the footprints are close enough together for students' strides. (Don't put the letters in alphabetical order or you'll get the "A B Cs" sung to you.) Choose a number of footprints appropriate for the skill level and attention span of your students. Some students are not ready to recognize all 26 letters at once or to wait in line very long for a turn.

2. Students form a line behind the first footprint.

3. The first student walks the footprints, saying each letter's name **before** it is stepped on, trying to get to the end without misnaming a letter. If a student does misname a letter, the teacher gives the correct letter name and lets the student continue, or has the student return to the end of the line and try again. (Some students may need to hold an adult's hand for balance as they walk the footsteps.)

4. When a student gets to the end of the footprints, he/she sits down to watch the next student in line.

Playing with Beginners

The teacher can walk beside a student as the footprints are stepped on. The teacher gives the name of the letter and has the student repeat it. It is best to practice only a few letters each time you play the game.

Advanced Play for Beginning Readers

Say the letter "sound" instead of the name as the footprints are walked on.

Variations

Color Walk

Using the pattern on page 10, cut footprints from colored construction paper or colored posterboard. Make one footprint for each color to be practiced.

Follow the basic directions on page 8 for playing the game.

Shape Walk

Reproduce the footprints on light brown construction paper. Glue one geometric shape on each footprint (see page 23 for shape patterns).

Follow the basic directions on page 8 for playing the game.

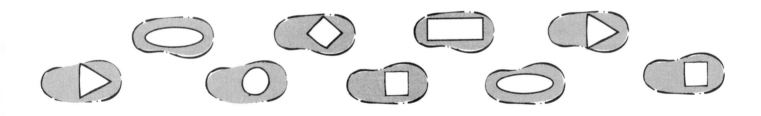

Note: Reproduce the footprint patterns to use with the game on page 7.

Patterns for Follow the Footprints

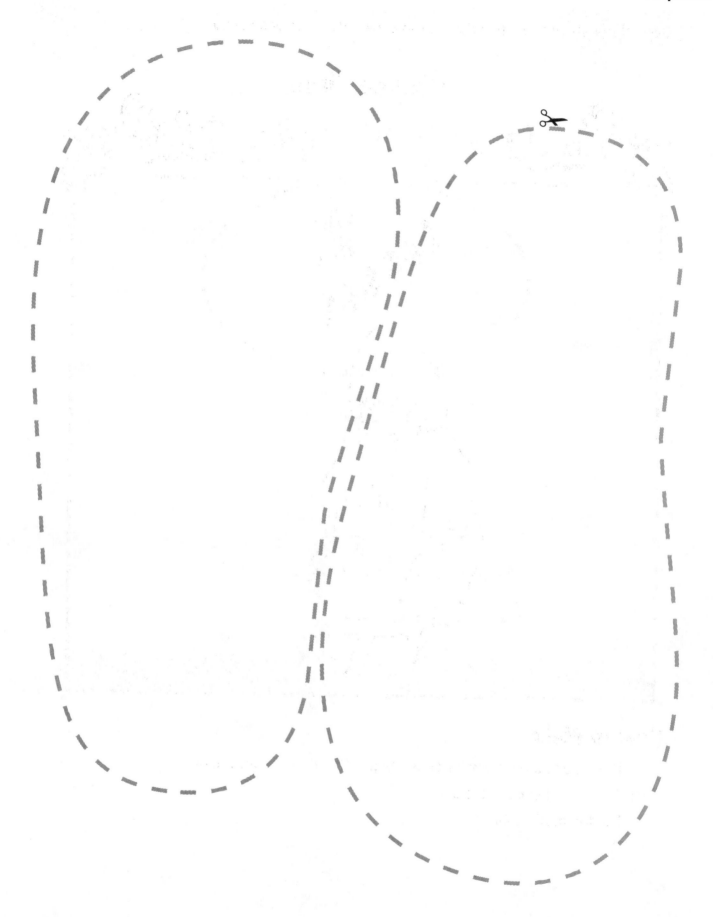

Language Games and Centers EMC 736

Rhyme Time

How to Make

1. Reproduce the picture cards on pages 15 - 18 on heavy paper.

2. Color and laminate the cards.

3. Cut the cards apart.

How to Play

1. Have students sit in a line facing the teacher.

2. Show each card to the group and say its name to be sure everyone can name the pictures. Give each student a card.

   (Have the cards divided so you keep one card from each rhyming pair.)

3. Show one of your cards to the group. Ask "Who has the card that rhymes with __?"

4. The student that has the rhyming card puts that card next to the teacher's card and says both words.

5. Play continues until all of the cards are matched.

Playing with Beginners

When rhyming is introduced, provide a lot of oral practice. Divide the picture cards into two sets, with one member of each rhyming pair in each set. Pass out one set of cards to the children. Show a card from the other set and say the picture name. Then put that card next to each student's card and say the two words. The students repeat both words and decide as a group if the words rhyme. When the rhyme is found, give the card to the student holding the rhyming word. Play continues until all the rhyming pairs have been formed. The game ends by having each student say his/her rhyming pair as the pictures are collected.

Advanced Play for More Skillful Players

As the students become more familiar with rhyming words, they can be asked to name more words that rhyme with their card when they place it next to the teacher's card. For example, if the teacher's card shows a cat, the student with the bat card places it next to the cat card and says" cat, bat, mat." Other players might also want to add to the list.

Advanced Play for Beginning Readers

Write the word on the back of the card when making the game. Then play the game using the word side of each card. If the student cannot read the word, he/she may look at the picture for assistance.

Variations

These variations help develop descriptive language and sentence usage.

Say a Sentence

Put the picture cards in a small sack. Each student selects a card and gives a complete sentence about it. If the student uses only a phrase, ask "Can you say that in a whole sentence?" If the student still has difficulty, teacher models the process. ("That is a funny frog.")

What Is It?

Place three of the pictures in a row. Model how to describe a picture without giving its name. ("This is a small green animal. It can hop. It eats bugs. What is it?") Students raise their hands if they know which picture is being described. Call on someone to pick up that picture card. Repeat the modeling process as needed for the particular group of students.

Put out three new cards and call on a volunteer to give a riddle. Continue until each student who wants a turn has had one.

Patterns for Rhyme Time

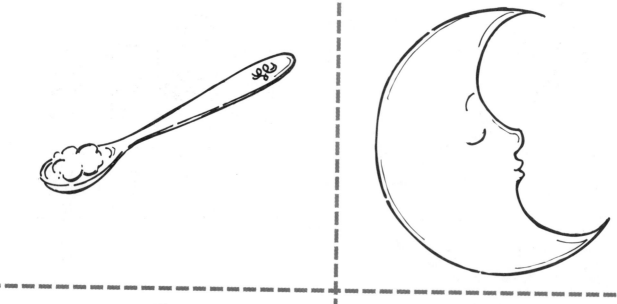

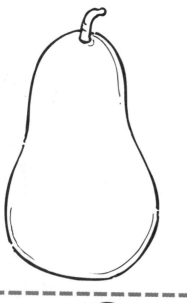

Language Games and Centers EMC 736

Note: Reproduce these picture cards to use with the game on page 12.

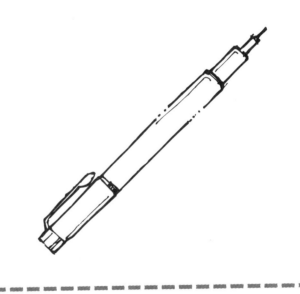

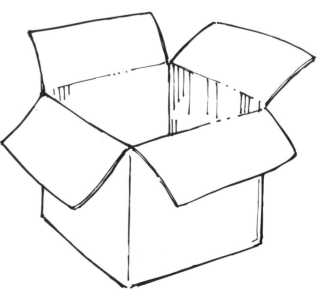

Language Games and Centers EMC 736

Patterns for Rhyme Time

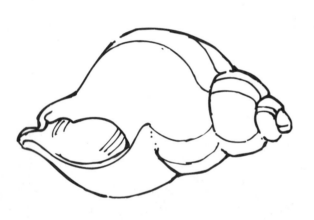

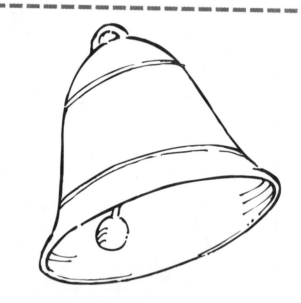

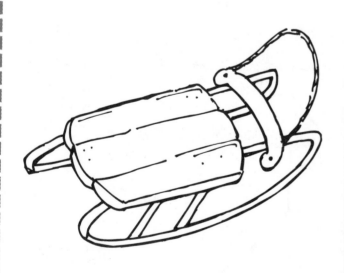

Roll the Cube

How to Make

1. You will need two half-gallon milk cartons and two different colors of Contact® paper to make one cube. (Or use two colors of construction paper and clear Contact® paper.)

continued on next page

2. Measure across the bottom of one milk carton. Measure the same distance up the sides of both cartons. Cut off the tops so you have squared off both the cartons. Push the two cartons together to form a cube.

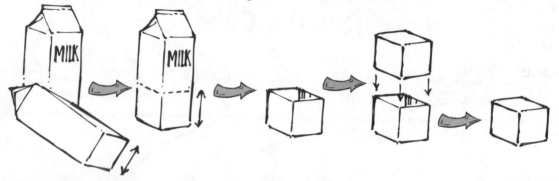

3. Cover the entire cube with colored Contact® paper or glue on construction paper.

4. Cut six different shapes (see page 23) out of another color of Contact® or construction paper. Fasten one shape to each side of the cube.

How to Play

1. Have students sit in a circle.

2. Give the cube to a student. The student will roll the cube toward the center of the circle and identify the shape that lands on top.

3. The cube is passed to the next student who rolls it and identifies the shape on top. Play continues until everyone has at least one turn.

This is a triangle. It has three sides.

Language Games and Centers EMC 736

Playing with Beginners

Play the game as described but have the group call out the shape name instead of having an individual student naming it. If your group isn't skilled enough to do this, have a student roll the cube, the teacher names the shape, and all the students repeat the name.

Advanced Play

Play the game as described above but have the student name the shape and then give one or two characteristics of that shape. Or have the student name the shape and then identify something in the classroom that has the same shape.

Variations

Make the cube following the instructions below and then play the game as described on page 20.

Colors

Use permanent felt markers to put a different colored circle or square on each side of the cube. (With students who are already reading, put the name of a color on each side of the cube.)

Nursery Rhymes

Put a different nursery rhyme picture on each side of the cube. (See page 26 for some examples.)

Have a student roll the cube. The student or the whole group recites the rhyme that is on top.

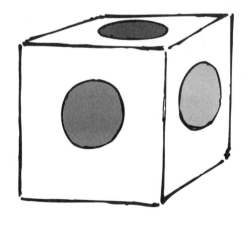

Categories

Put a picture of something to represent a different category on each side of the cube. (See pages 24 and 25 for some pictures you might use.) You will need six pictures for each cube.

A student rolls the cube and names a category in which the object in the picture might belong. Extend the activity in one of these ways:

1. The student that rolled the cube says the category and then names something else in that category.

2. After the student has named the category, each student in the circle names something else that goes in that category before the cube is rolled again.

Some ideas for categories and pictures:

Pictures	Categories
dog or cat	pets or animals
cow or horse	animals or farm animals
apple or banana	fruit or food
chicken	bird or farm animal
shoe	clothing or something to wear on feet
chair	furniture or something to sit on
pencil	school thing or something to write with
ball	toy
stove	something found in a kitchen or something to cook with

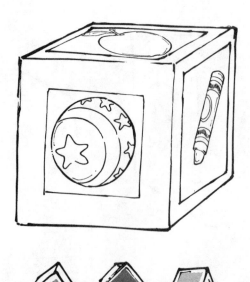

Note: Reproduce the geometric patterns to use with the game on page 19.

Patterns for Basic Shapes

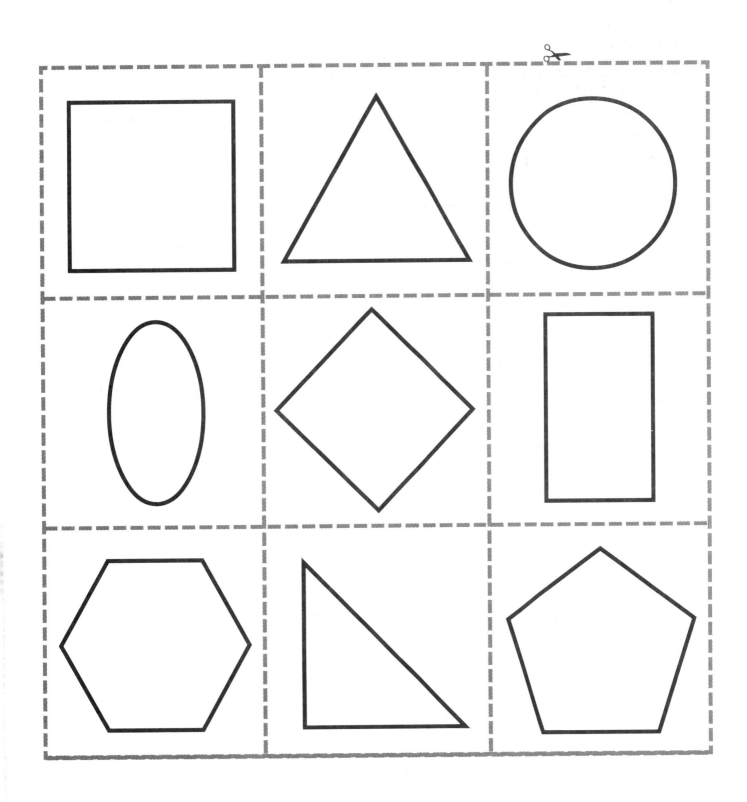

Patterns for Roll the Cube

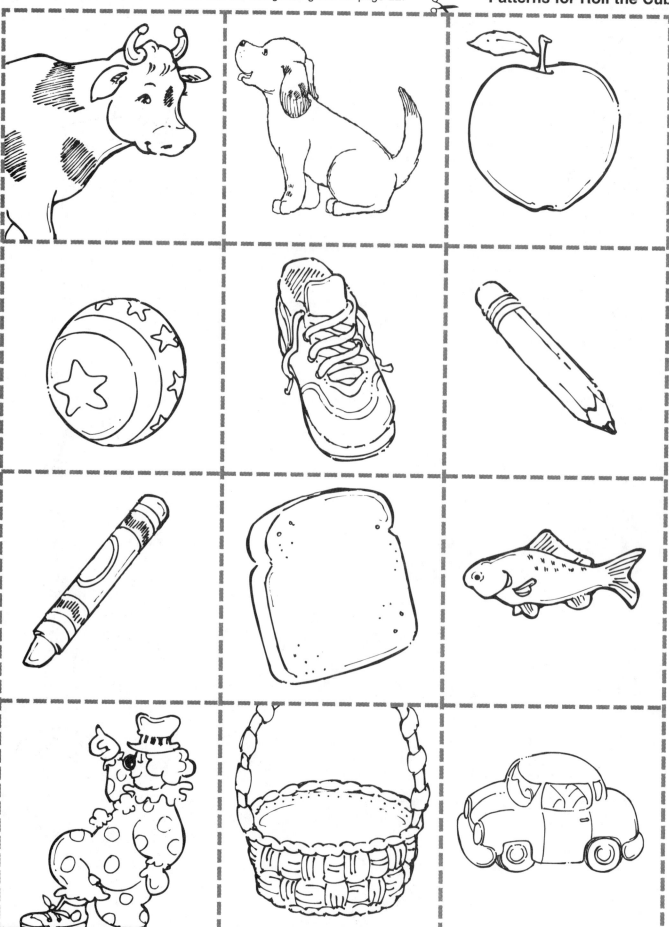

Patterns for Roll the Cube

Patterns for Roll the Cube

Let's Go Fishing

How to Make

1. Make fish.

    a. Reproduce the fish on pages 30 - 36 on orange construction paper.
    (If you wish to practice only capital or lower case letters, use the blank patterns on page 36. Reproduce a fish for each letter you wish to practice. Write one letter on each fish.)

    b. Laminate the fish.

    c. Cut out the fish and put a paper clip on the "mouth" of each fish.

continued on next page

2. Make a pond.
   Cut a "pond" shape from blue butcher paper.

3. Make a fishing pole.

   You will need:

   - a smooth stick about three feet (one meter) long
     (doweling, yardstick, meterstick, etc.)

   - a piece of string about one yard (one meter) long

   - a magnet powerful enough to pick up a fish

Tie or tape the string to one end of the stick and the magnet to the other end.

How to Play

1. Have students sit in a circle around the "pond."

2. Put the fish in the pond. The fish may be letter-side up so students can choose the letter they want or letter-side down so they are surprised by their catch.

3. The fisherman stands holding the pole and "catches" (pulls up) a fish by touching the paper clip with the magnet and then names the letter on the fish. If the letter is named correctly, the fisherman keeps the fish. If it is misnamed, the teacher says the letter name and the fish is returned to the pond.

4. Students take turns until all the fish are caught.

Playing with Beginners

When the fisherman catches a fish, the teacher says the letter name, the student repeats it and keeps the fish. After all the fish are caught, they are returned to the pond one at a time as the teacher says "Let the **A** fish go," "Let the **B** fish go," etc.

Advanced Play for Beginning Readers

Use the game to practice letter sounds instead of letter names. Fishermen give the sound of the letter on each fish they catch.

M says
m m m.

Variations

Use the fishing game to practice other skills. Make the fish following the directions below. Then play the game following the directions on page 27.

Fish for Colors

Cut the fish from colored construction paper or posterboard. Make several fish in each color if the game is to be played by several students. Place a paper clip on the front of each fish.

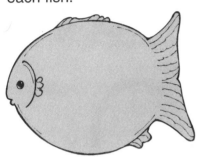 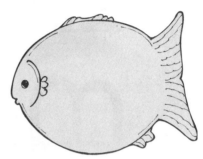 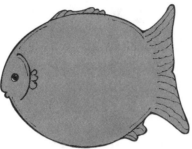

For beginning readers make a set of fish using white construction paper or posterboard. Write the color names on the fish. Place a paper clip on the front of each fish.

 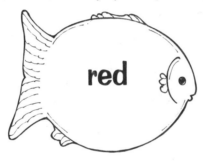 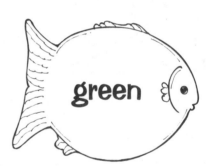

Fish for Shapes

Reproduce and cut out the fish containing geometric shapes (pages 37 - 38). Place a paper clip on the front of each fish.

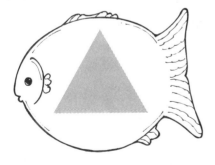 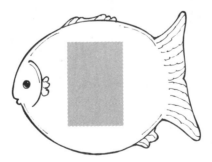 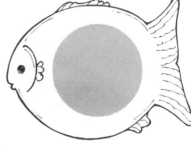

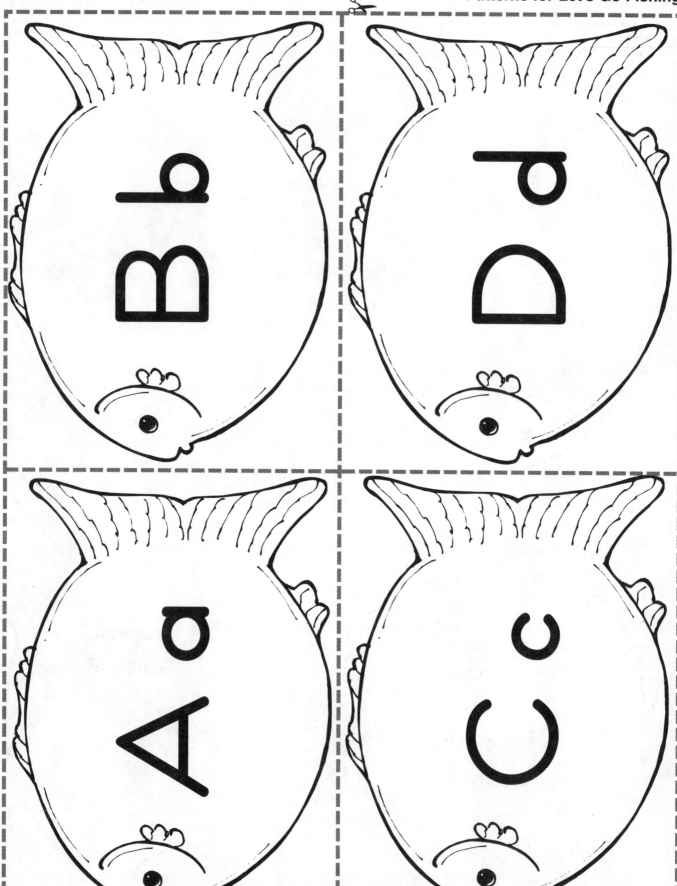

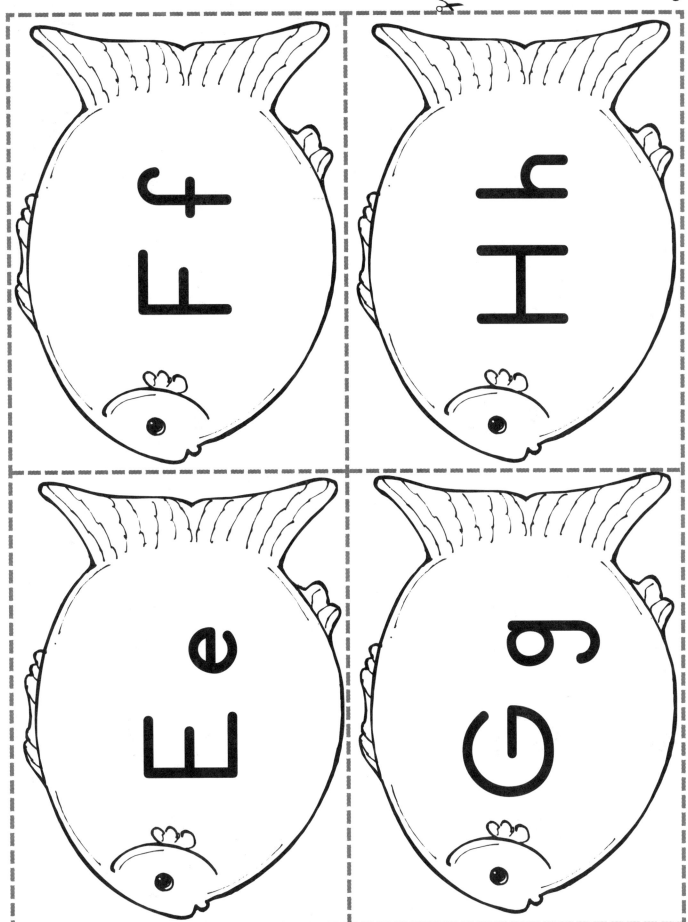

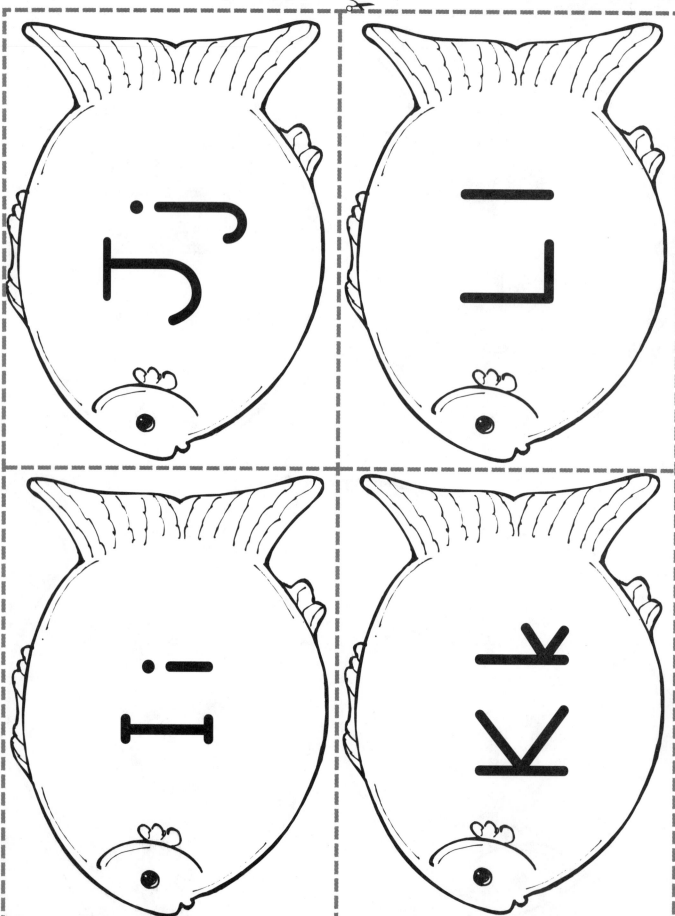

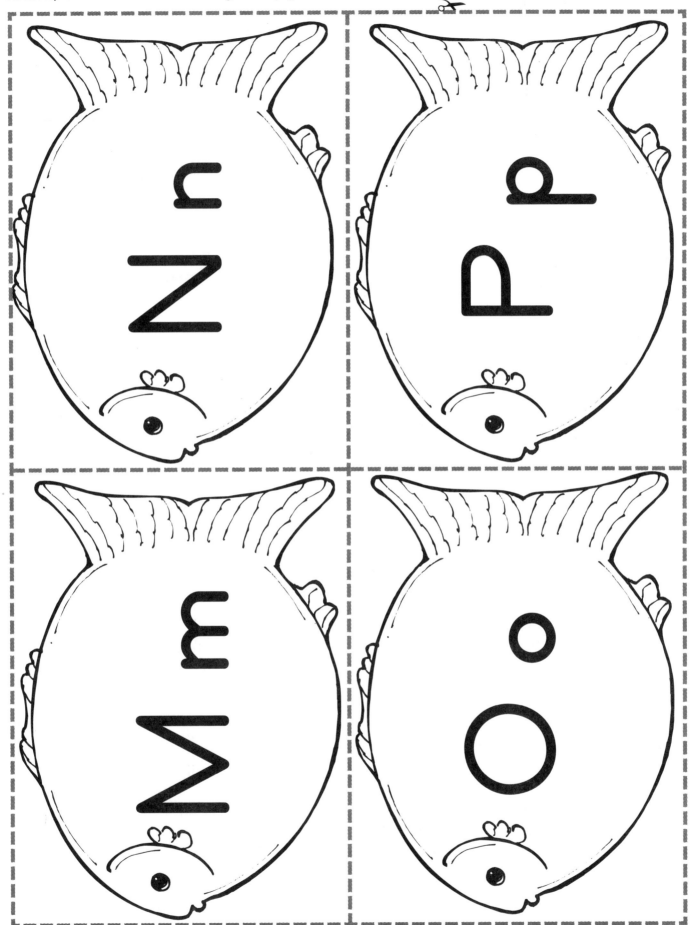

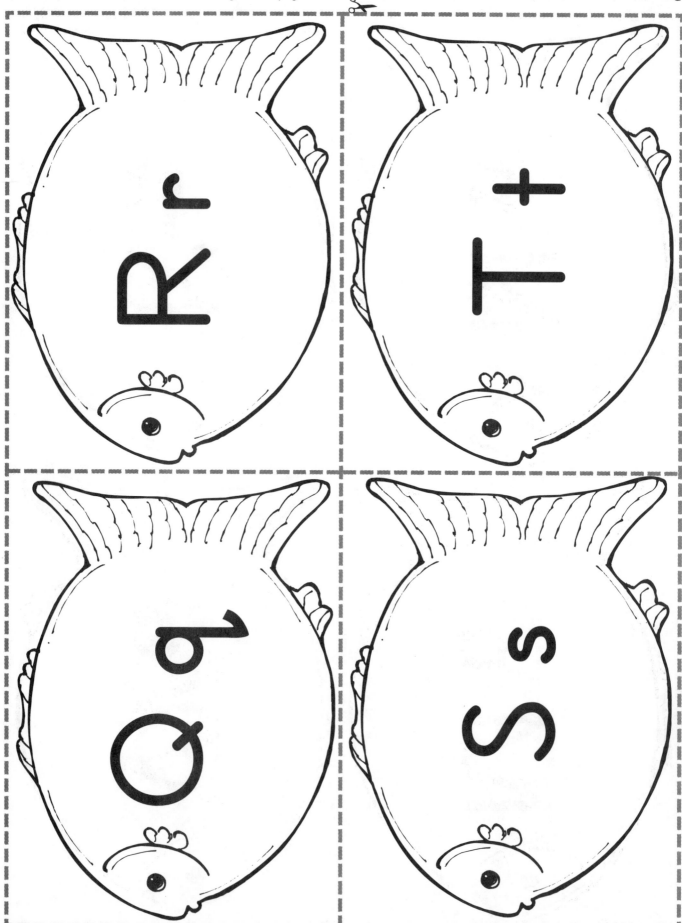

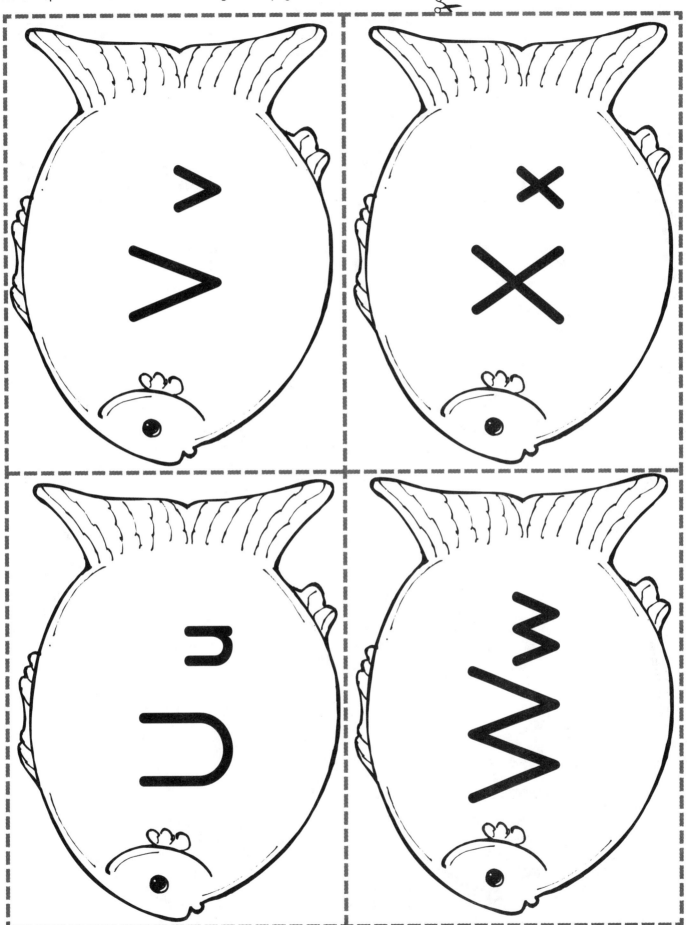

Language Games and Centers EMC 736

Z z

Y y

Note: Reproduce the fish to use with the shape game on page 29.

Patterns for Let's Go Fishing

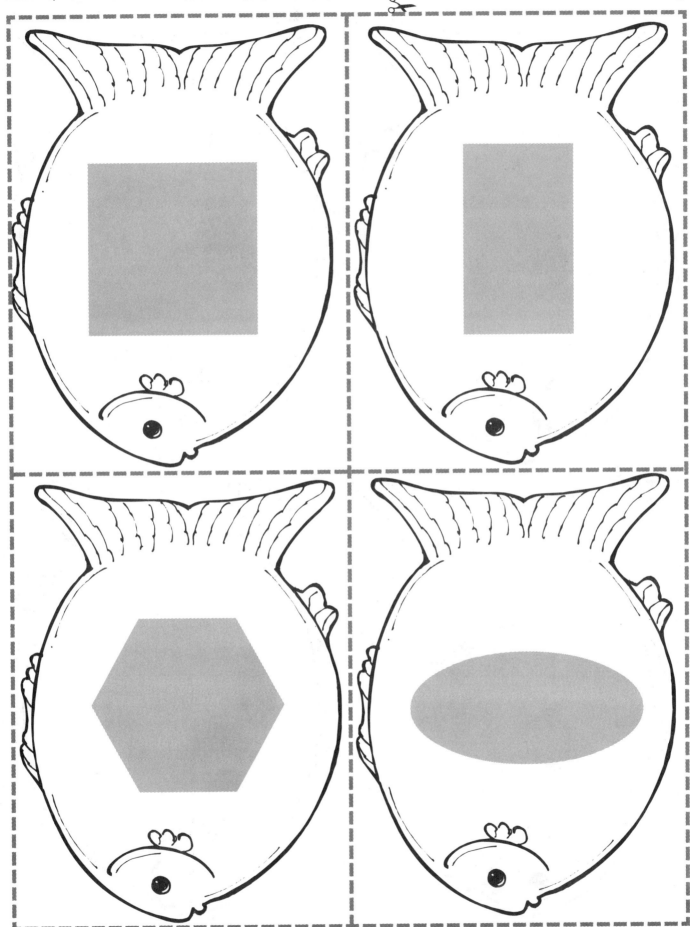

Language Games and Centers EMC 736

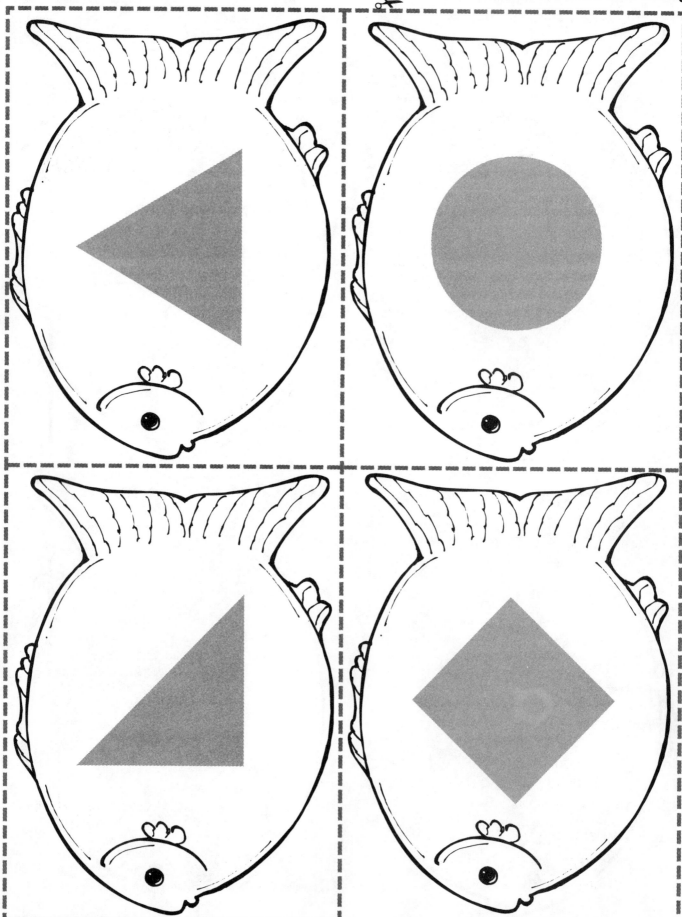

Where's the Bear?

How to Make

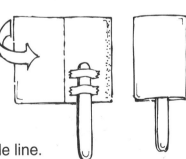

1. Reproduce the bear pattern on page 41 on white paper. You will need one bear per player.

2. Color the bear.

3. Laminate the bear.

4. Cut out the bear pattern and fold in half on the middle line.

5. Glue or tape a tongue depressor inside. Glue the two halves together.

How to Play

Give each student a bear puppet. The students ask "Where's the bear?" The teacher replies by telling the students the bear's location using a positional word ("He is **over** your head," "He is **under** your chin," "He is in your **right** hand"). The students hold their bears where the teacher has directed. The game continues as time and interest allow.

It is helpful to keep a list of position words or actual directions on a card to avoid having to ad lib. A list will also assist a parent or aide to play the game with the students.

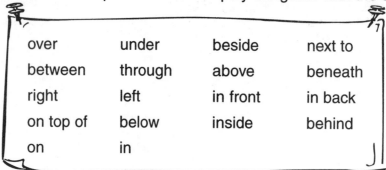

over	under	beside	next to
between	through	above	beneath
right	left	in front	in back
on top of	below	inside	behind
on	in		

Playing with Beginners

Teacher begins by telling and showing the students where he/she is putting the bear. ("My bear is **over** my head.") Students copy the teacher who then asks, "Where's your bear?" The students repeat what teacher told them. ("My bear is **over** my head.")

Advanced Play

Only the teacher has a bear. The teacher holds the bear in a position and asks, "Where's the bear?" The students respond by giving the location shown by the teacher. ("He's over your head," etc.)

Where's the bear?

Pattern for Where's the Bear?

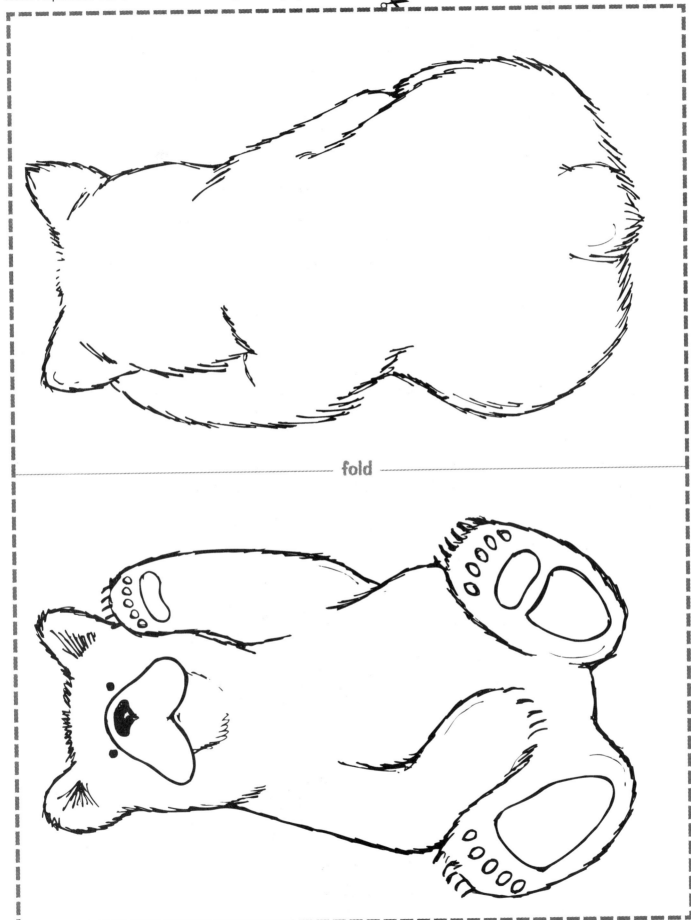

fold

Heart Concentration

How to Make

1. Reproduce the hearts on pages 45 - 49. Make two copies of each page. (You will need two hearts for each letter you want to practice.)

   Reproduce the blank hearts on page 49 and write on the letters to practice:
   - Capital and lower case letters together on a heart.
   - Capital letters alone.
   - Matching capital letters with lower case letters.

2. Laminate the hearts.

3. Cut out the hearts.

How to Play

1. Have students sit in a line facing the cards.

2. Place the heart cards letter-side down in two or three lines in front of the students. Use only 10 or 12 cards at a time with beginners (five or six different letter pairs). Increase the number of cards as students' skills and memories develop.

3. The first student turns over two cards and calls out the name of the letter on each. (If the student misses the letter, the teacher says the letter name.) If the two letters match the student takes the two hearts. If the letters don't match, the hearts are turned back over in the same place. The play advances to the next player.

4. Play continues until all of the hearts are gone.

Play with Skilled Players

Use a set of hearts which have the capital on one heart and the lower case on the other. A match consists of the capital and lower case letters.

Advanced Play for Beginning Readers

Players say the letter and letter sound as hearts are turned over.

Variations

Make a set of hearts following the directions below. Play each game following the rules for concentration on page 43.

Color Concentration

Cut hearts from pink construction paper. Glue a piece of the same color construction paper on pairs of pink hearts. Laminate and cut out the hearts. Place hearts pink side up and play to find same-color pairs.

Heart Match

Use the same hearts made for the letter matching game on page 43 to play with a large group. You will need one heart per student, making sure to have two matching pairs. If there are an odd number of students, the teacher plays, too.

1. Mix up the hearts and pass them out at random.

2. Have students walk around the room until they find their matching partners. The partners sit down together.

3. When all are seated, the teacher says, "Bring me the **a** hearts." The students with **a** give the their hearts to the teacher. Continue until all of the hearts are collected.

a

b

c

d

e

f

g

h

i

j

k

l

m

n

o

p

q

r

Patterns for Heart Concentration

s

t

u

v

w

x

Patterns for Heart Concentration

y

z

49

Same or Different?

How to Make

There are no materials to make. You will use the students themselves or use real objects from around the classroom to play this game.

Categories of comparison might include:

shape	size	function	texture	taste
sound	color	composition	smell	living/nonliving

Language Games and Centers EMC 736

How to Play

1. Have students sit in a line facing the teacher.

2. Place two objects (or have two students stand) in front of the students.

3. Ask "What is the same about the these two objects (or these two students)?" Then ask "What is different about these two objects (or these two students)?"

   You may need to prompt the students by asking questions such as, "Which is bigger?", "Are they the same shape?", etc.

4. As the students become better at making comparisons, have them look at three or more objects or people and tell the likenesses and differences they see.

What is the same about Anna and Michael?

Variations

Big, Bigger, Biggest (or Small, Smaller, Smallest)

Use three objects that differ only in size. Select a student to arrange the objects in order of size. Remove one object from sight. Ask "Which of these two is bigger?" ("Which is smaller?") Return the item and have the students tell you once again which is big, bigger, biggest (or small, smaller, smallest).

Tall, Taller, Tallest (or Short, Shorter, Shortest)

Have three students of varying heights line up. Have the rest of the group tell who is tallest and who is shortest. Replace either the tallest or the shortest student with someone else. Have students decide who is tallest and shortest now. This game can be varied by using only two students (taller/shorter) or having more than three line up.

First to Last (Ordinal Number Practice)

Have several students line up in a row. Ask "Who is first in line?" and "Who is last in line?" Have everyone in line turn and face the opposite directions. Ask "Now who is first?" and "Now who is last?"

Count Off (Ordinal Number Practice)

Have five students line up in a row. Have the students count off: "First, second, third, fourth, fifth." Then ask "Who is second in line?", "Who is fifth?", etc. Have the line turn to face the opposite direction. Count off again and repeat the questions.

This variation can also be played with real objects, stuffed animals, or pictures (see pages 53 and 54). Color, cut out, and glue the pictures to tagboard. Line them up in the chalktray. (Or put a piece of Velcro® on the back of each picture and place them on a flannelboard.)

Patterns for Count Off

Language Games and Centers EMC 736

Note: Reproduce the picture cards to use with "Count Off" on page 52.

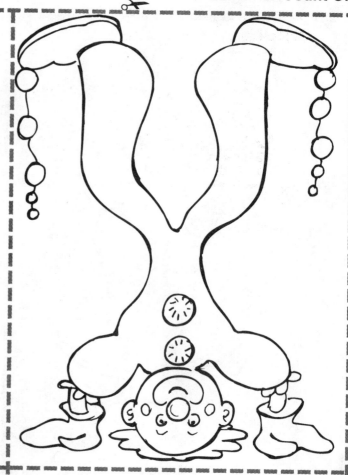

Language Games and Centers EMC 736

The Ice Cream Cone Game

(up to six players)

How to Make

1. Reproduce the cone patterns on pages 58 and 59.

2. Reproduce the picture "scoops" on pages 60 and 61.

3. Color, laminate, and cut out the cones and scoops.

How to Play

1. Students sit in a line facing the teacher.

2. Lay the cones in a row in front of the teacher. (Have the pictures pointing toward the students.)

3. Pass out a scoop of ice cream to each student. Ask one student at a time to put their ice cream scoop on the cone it rhymes with. As they put the ice cream on the cone have them tell why it goes there. ("This is a tree. It rhymes with bee.")

4. If a student has difficulty finding the correct cone, have him/her lay the ice cream scoop by each cone and say both picture names until the rhyme is located ("bee-clown, bee-star, bee-tree).

5. Play continues until all cones have two ice cream scoops.

Play with Beginners

A great deal of oral rhyming practice is needed before children can be successful playing rhyming games.

One student is called up to stand by the teacher. The teacher holds an ice cream scoop by each cone and says both picture names. The student stops the teacher when a rhyme is made and takes the scoop to place on the correct cone. (If this is too difficult for an individual, have the group decides which words rhyme.)

Advanced Play for More Skillful Players

As the students become more familiar with rhyming words they can be asked to name more words that rhyme with their card match. For example, if the ice cream cone says bee, the student with the tree card places it on the cone and says "knee, me, she, key, etc." Other players might add to the list also.

Advanced Play for Beginning Readers

Write CVC words that rhyme on the blank cones and ice cream scoops on pages 62 and 63. Play the game in the same way.

Words you might use:

Patterns for The Ice Cream Cone Game

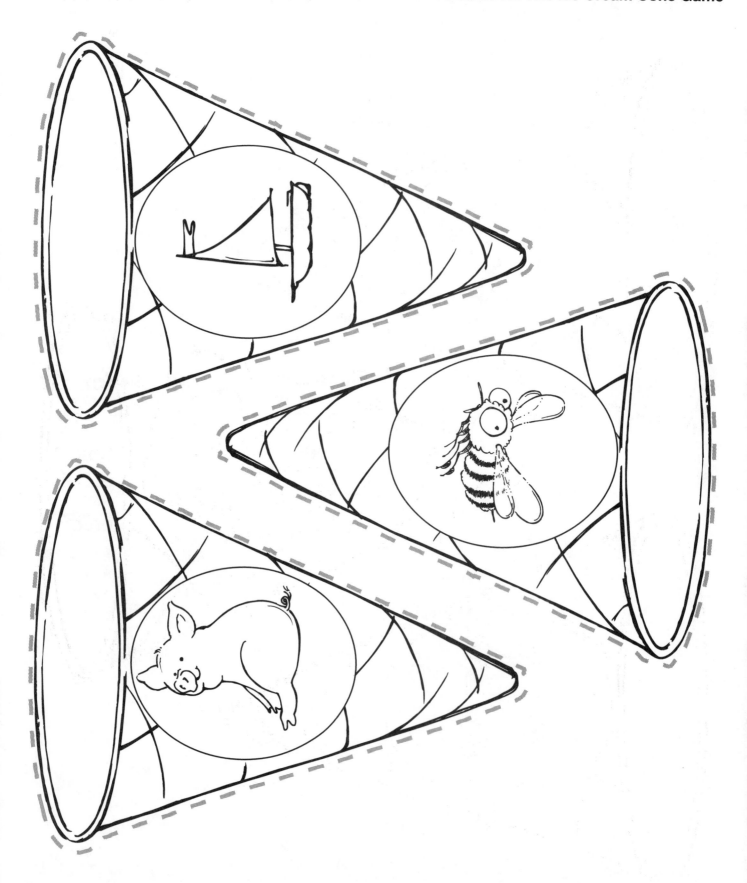

Patterns for The Ice Cream Cone Game

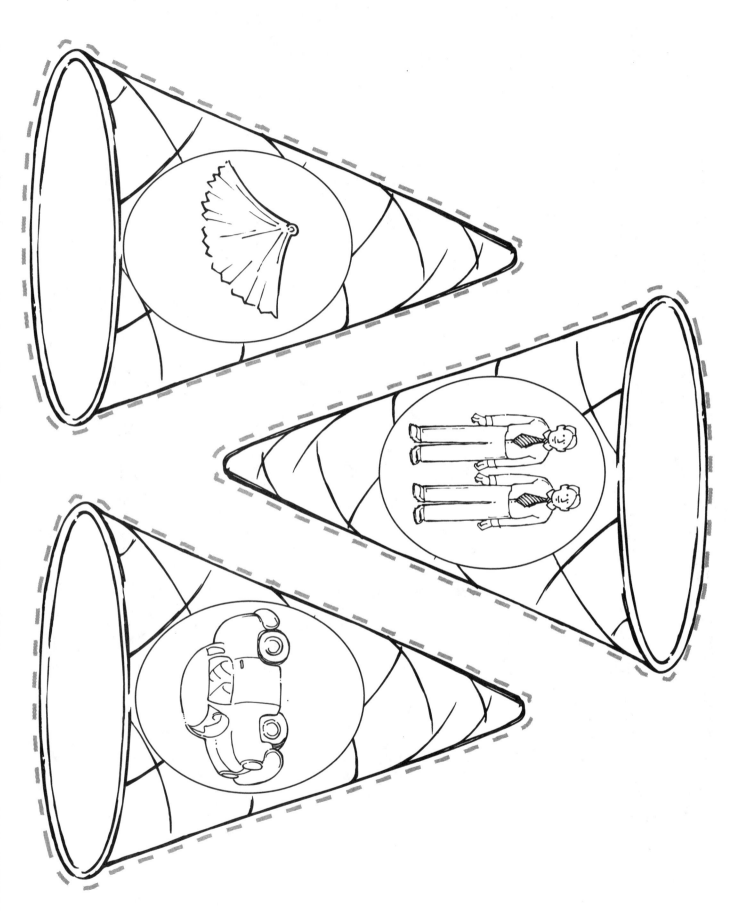

Language Games and Centers EMC 736

Patterns for The Ice Cream Cone Game

Patterns for The Ice Cream Cone Game

Language Games and Centers EMC 736

Patterns for The Ice Cream Cone Game

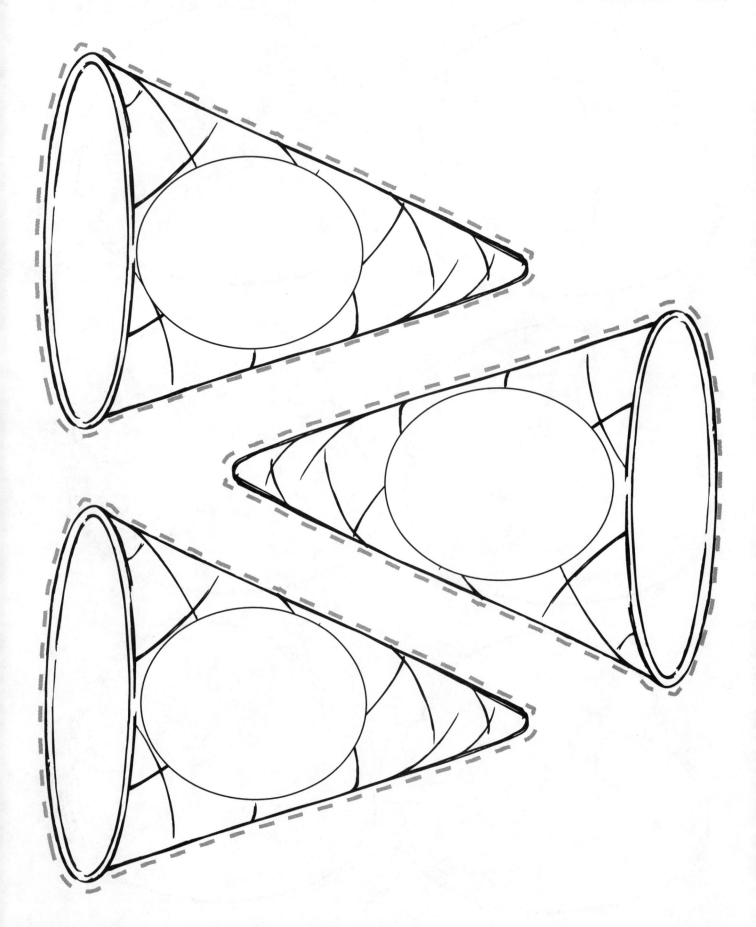

Patterns for The Ice Cream Cone Game

Language Games and Centers EMC 736

5-in-a-Row

How to Make

1. Reproduce the "5-in-a-Row" form on page 67. You'll need one playing sheet per student.

2. Print the letters of the alphabet on each sheet in a random order. You'll have 25 spaces, so you will need to eliminate one letter. (X is a good one to eliminate as it is infrequently used and is easily recognized by most students. Be sure no two sheets are exactly alike.

3. Reproduce the letter cards on pages 70 - 72 (or use 3" x 5" [7.5 x 13 cm] index cards and print a different letter on each card). These will be your calling cards.

4. Cut a lot of 1" (2.5 cm) square pieces of construction paper to use as markers to cover the letters as they are called. Beans and buttons can be used with older students, but paper is safer as students can't choke on it as easily.

How to Play

1. Give each student a playing sheet and some markers. Be sure all players can see the letter cards as they are shown.

2. Teacher shuffles the calling cards and puts them in a stack face down. She/He turns over the top card and says its name.

3. Students put a marker on the letter called where it appears on their playing sheets. The teacher continues to call letters until a student gets five in a row vertically, horizontally, or diagonally. The student calls out "5 in a Row" to indicate he/she has a complete row.

3. Use the discard pile to check the student's playing sheet to see if all letters are correct.

4. At this point you can start over or continue playing until another student gets "5 in a Row."

Playing with Beginners

Show students the card as you say the name and hold it up while they are looking for the letter on their playing sheets.

Advanced Play for Beginning Readers

Make a set of calling cards with pictures cut from magazines or duplicate some of the pictures used with other games in this book. Make one card for each letter of the alphabet except X, as it does not occur on the playing sheets. Play in the same way, but tell students to find the letter that makes the sound with which the picture begins.

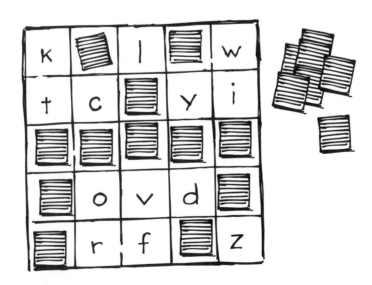

Variations

Use 5-in-a-Row, 4-in-a-Row (page 68), or 3-in-a-Row (page 69) playing sheets, which-ever is more appropriate for the amount of colors, shapes, or numerals you wish to practice.

1. Prepare and play the same as for letters, but substitute shapes or colors for the letters on the playing sheets.

2. Reproduce the appropriate calling cards for shapes (see page 23 for shape patterns). Make colored squares or dots on the playing sheets to practice color recognition.

3. Remember to put the colors or shapes in random order and to make each playing sheet different.

Play following the rules for the game on page 65.

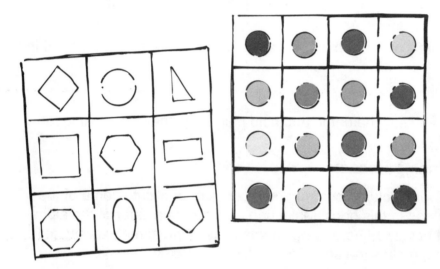

6	2	10	20	7
12	16	3	4	18
5	15	25	11	21
13	1	22	9	19
23	14	8	17	24

Language Games and Centers EMC 736

Note: Reproduce the form to use with the game on page 64.

5-in-a-Row

Note: Reproduce this form to use with the game on page 66.

 # 4-in-a-Row

68

Note: Reproduce this form to use with the game on page 66.

 # 3-in-a-Row

Note: Reproduce these letter cards to use with the game on page 64.

Patterns for 5-in-a-Row

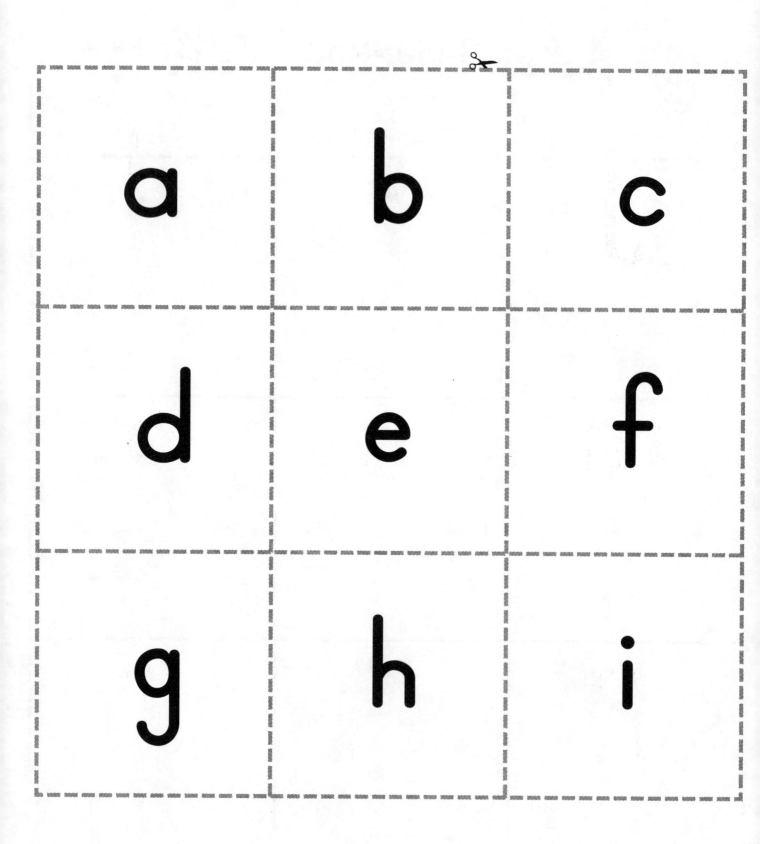

Note: Reproduce these letter cards to use with the game on page 64.

Patterns for 5-in-a-Row

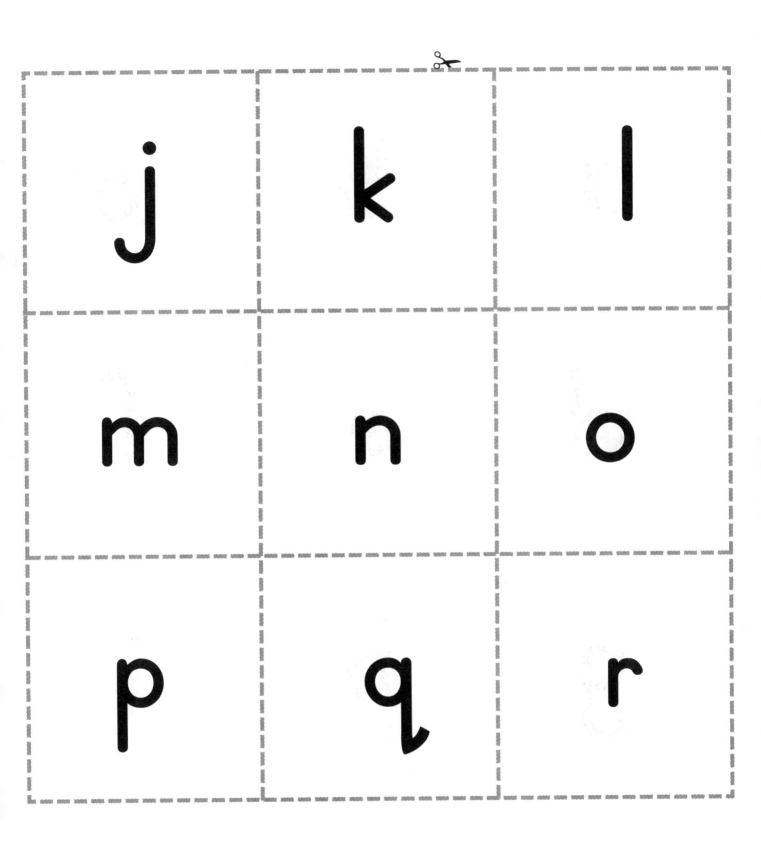

Note: Reproduce these letter cards to use with the game on page 64.

Patterns for 5-in-a-Row

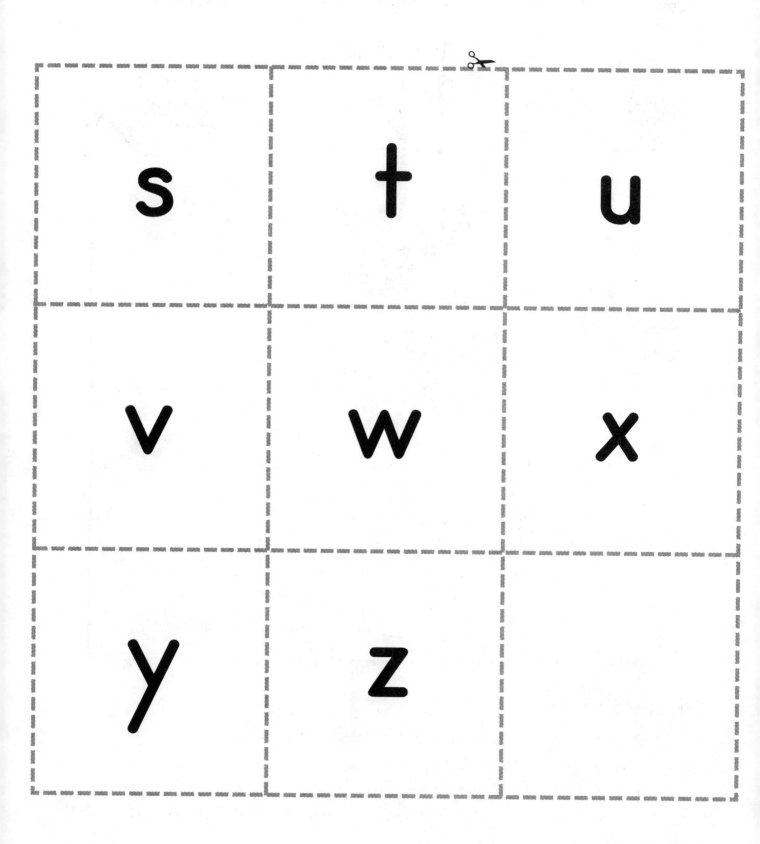

s	t	u
v	w	x
y	z	

Ask or Tell?

How to Make

1. Reproduce the asking and telling face patterns on page 76.

2. Color and cut out the patterns.

3. Take two lunch-sized paper bags. Paste one face on each bag.

4. Put several small items into each bag. Be sure to have at least one item per person playing the game.

How to Play

1. Have students sit in a line facing the teacher. The two bags are placed in front of the teacher.

2. Teacher explains to the students what each face represents and models a "telling" sentence and an "asking" sentence.

3. A student selects an object out of either bag. If the object comes from the "tell" bag, the student makes a statement about the object using a complete sentence. (For example, "This is a blue crayon" or "You use a crayon to color a picture.") If the object is from the "ask" bag, the student asks a question about it. (For example, "What color is this crayon?" or "Do you like to draw with a blue crayon?")

4. After making the statement or question, the student puts the object into the opposite bag so if it is taken by another student, the same type of sentence isn't repeated. (Or remove the object from the game once it has been used.)

5. Play continues until all students have had a turn.

Playing with Beginners

The teacher needs to explain the difference between asking and telling. Start by modeling each sentence form. Say "I'm going to tell you something about this—this is a blue crayon." Then put it into the "tell" bag. Take it back out and say "Now I'm going to ask you something about this—what color is this crayon?" Put it into the "ask" bag. Repeat this until students understand that a question (ask) requires an answer, but a statement (tell) doesn't. Let students try a few sentences with your help.

Advanced Play for More Skillful Players

1. Have the objects in front of the empty bags. A student selects an object and makes either a statement or asks a question about it. Then the student puts the object into the correct bag.

2. Have the objects in front of the empty bags. A student selects an object and calls on another student who makes a statement or asks a question about the object. The student who selected the object must decide if the second student ask or told about the object and place it in the correct bag.

This is a blue crayon.

Patterns for Ask or Tell

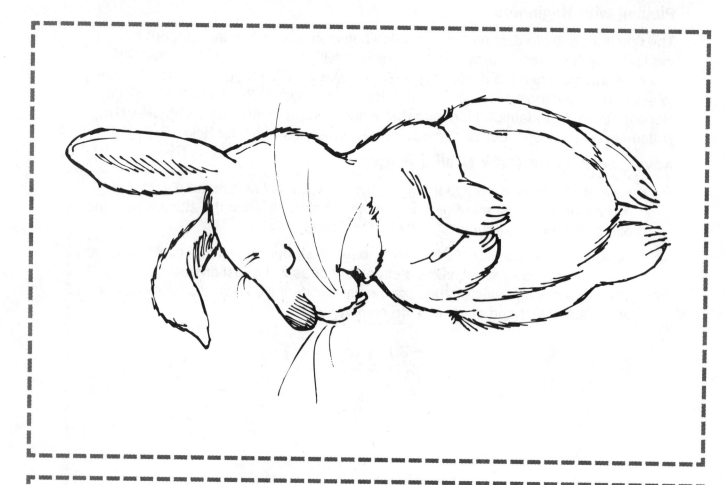

The Watermelon Game

How to Make

1. Reproduce the watermelon slice patterns on pages 79 and 80 on red construction paper. You will need 26 copies of the plain slice and 10 copies of the slice with seeds.

2. Paint a green "rind" on each slice. You may color or paint the seeds black if you wish.

3. Print a different letter, both capital and lower case, on each of the plain slices.

4. Laminate and cut out the watermelon slices.

77

How to Play

1. Have students sit in a circle.

2. Mix up the watermelon slices with letters. Insert a slice with seeds every two or three letters. These will be used to signal a change of turn.

3. Place the slices face down in the middle of the circle. Have one student begin play by turning over the top slice and naming the letter written on it. If the letter is named correctly, the student keeps the watermelon slice and turns over another slice. Play continues until the student cannot identify the letter or until a slice with seeds is picked. (If the student doesn't know the letter name or misnames it, the teacher gives the correct name and slips that slice back into the pile.)

   Play moves on to the next student. (If the students in the group have short attention spans, have each student pick only one slice. If seeds are picked, every one says "seeds" and the play moves on. Eventually everyone will get a letter card.)

4. Continue around the circle until all of the slices are in front of students, or until all of the students have had an equal number of turns.

Play with Beginners

Play the game without the seed slices. The first student selects a slice. The teacher says the letter name and the student repeats it and keeps the slice. Play moves on to the next player.

Advanced Play for Beginning Readers

Have students take watermelon slices and give the letter sound instead of the letter name.

Language Games and Centers EMC 736

Note: Reproduce the pattern to use with the game on page 77.

Pattern for The Watermelon Game

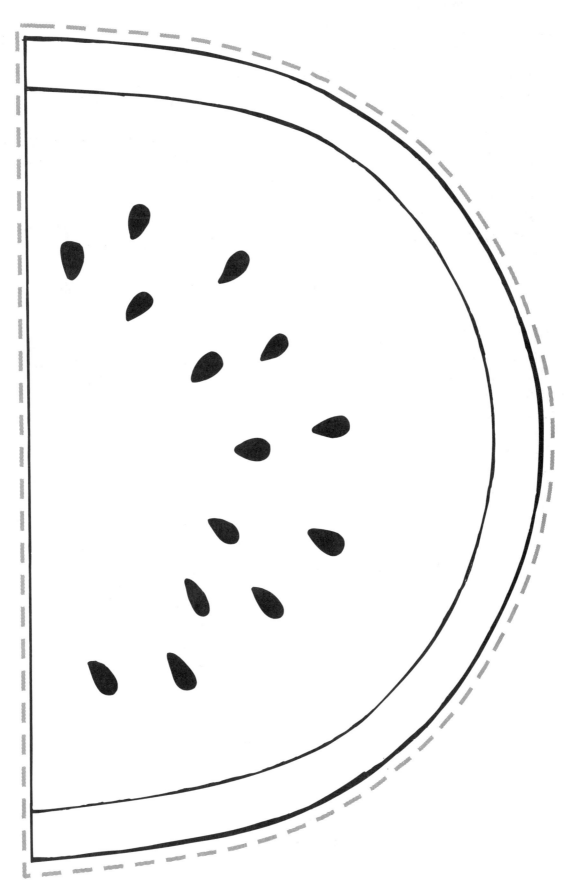

Language Games and Centers EMC 736

Pattern for The Watermelon Game

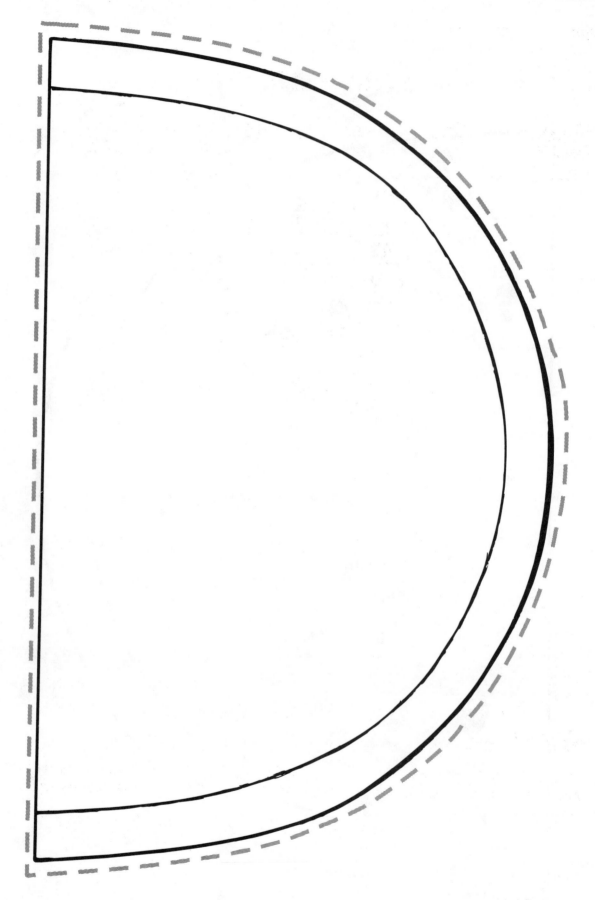

What's Missing?

How to Make

There's nothing to make for this game! You just need to collect several small items from around the classroom. For example, eraser, paper clip, pencil, crayons, die, paper scrap, button, scissors, etc.

         Language Games and Centers EMC 736

How to Play

1. Have the students sit in a circle.

2. Place items in the middle of the circle. (Use only three to five items for beginners and six to ten with more advanced players.) Point to each item and name it before play begins.

3. Give the students a moment to study the items. Then have them close their eyes and cover them with their hands, or turn their backs while an item is removed.

4. Ask, "What's missing?" The students look at the items and say what they think was taken away.

5. When students have guessed correctly, show them the item, put it back in the center of the circle, and continue play.

Advanced Play

- Include several items that are the same except for their color and/or size (a big blue button, a small white button, and a button with a flower on it). This requires students to describe items, not just to name them.

- Remove two or more items at the same time. This makes it more difficult to remember.

- Play "What's Different?" by changing the position of an item rather than removing it. Students have to tell what was moved and where it was originally placed.

Variations

Collect or make playing pieces as described below. Play using the same rules as on page 82. The games are listed in ascending order of difficulty.

Color

Use crayons or construction paper scraps as the items being removed.

Shape

Use shapes cut from one color of construction paper as the items being removed. (See shape patterns on page 23.)

Color and Shape

Use shapes cut from various colors of construction paper as the items being removed. For example, a blue triangle, a red triangle, a green circle, and orange circle, etc.

Color, Shape, and Size

Use shapes cut from various colors of construction paper in two sizes. For example, a big blue triangle, a small blue triangle, etc.

Apple Match

How to Make

1. Reproduce the apples on pages 87 - 95 on red construction paper.

2. Laminate the apples.

3. Cut out the apples.

How to Play

1. Have students sit in a line.

2. Lay the apples with the capital letters on them face-up in a line in front of the students. Start with 5-6 apples. Gradually add more as students become skilled at the game. Place the apples in alphabetical order at first. As students become more skillful, mix up the apples.

3. Give each student an apple containing a lower case letter. Each student in turn places the lower case apple under its matching capital letter.

4. Continue passing out lower case apples until all are matched or until all students have had an equal number of turns.

Vary the game by putting out the lower case letters and have students match the capital forms.

Advanced Play

Mix capital and lower case letters in the same line. Be sure to lay out only one from each pair of letters.

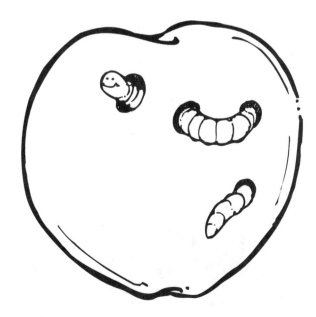

                                       Language Games and Centers EMC 736

Variations

Letter Identification

Use the same set of apples prepared for the Apple Match game. Reproduce "wormy apples" on page 95. Play the game in the same way as The Watermelon Game on page 78. (The wormy apples are used in the same way as the watermelons with seeds.)

Alphabetical Order

Use either the capital or the lower case apples for this activity. Pass out all the apples (students will have more than one). Ask "What is the first letter of the alphabet?" Have the student with that letter bring it up. Ask "Which letter comes after (a)?" Have that letter brought up and placed after the "a" apple. Continue until the whole alphabet is complete.

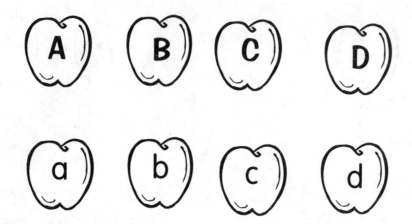

Language Games and Centers EMC 736

Note: Reproduce the apple forms to use with the game on page 84.

Patterns for Apple Match

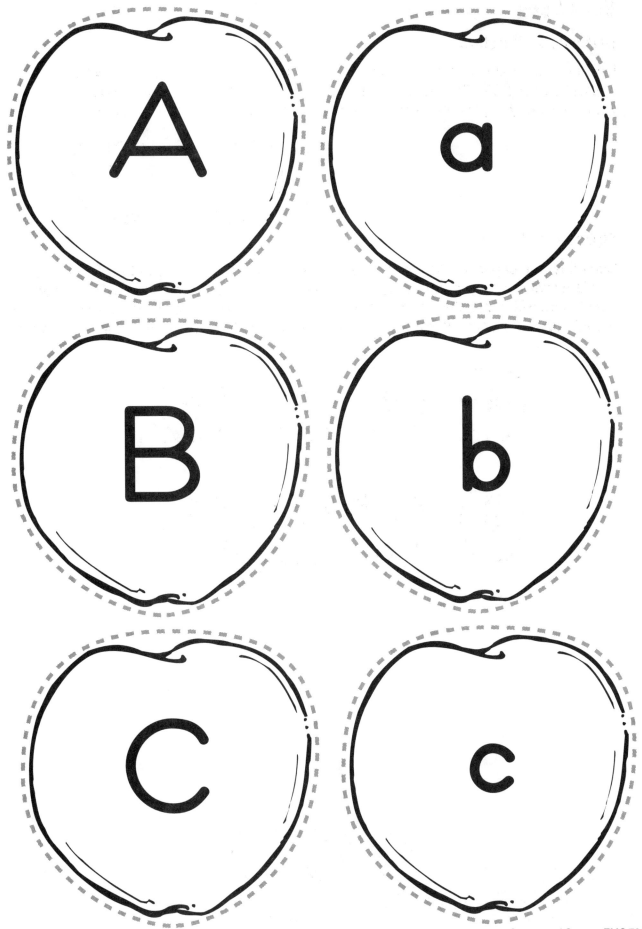

Note: Reproduce the apple forms to use with the game on page 84.

Patterns for Apple Match

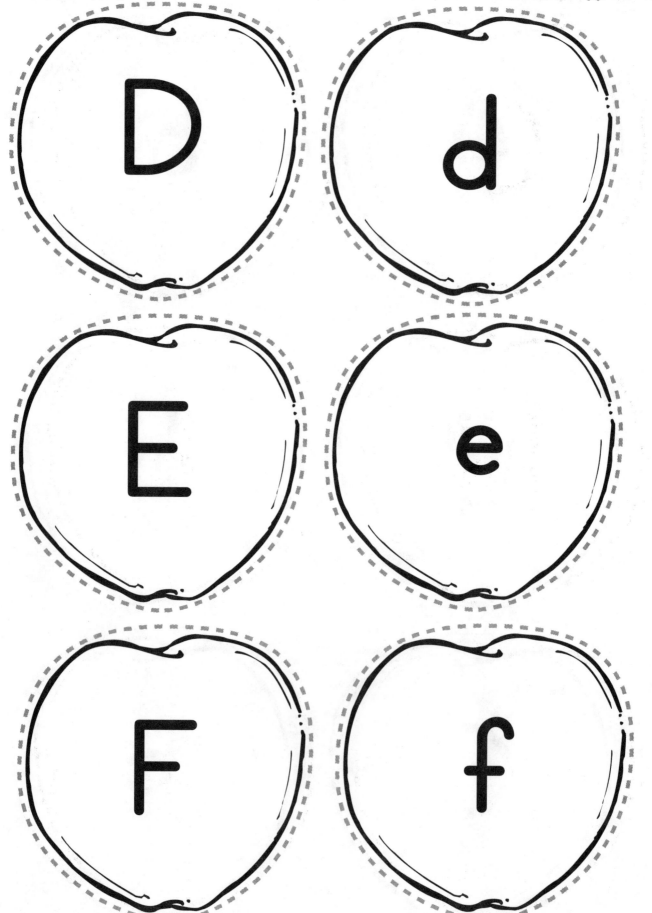

Note: Reproduce the apple forms to use with the game on page 84.

Patterns for Apple Match

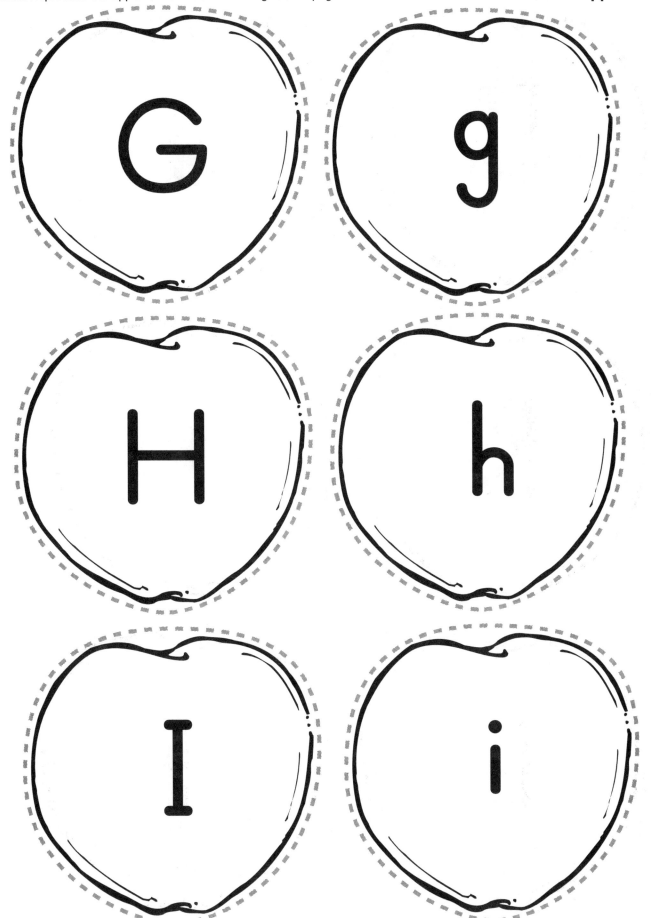

Note: Reproduce the apple forms to use with the game on page 84.

Patterns for Apple Match

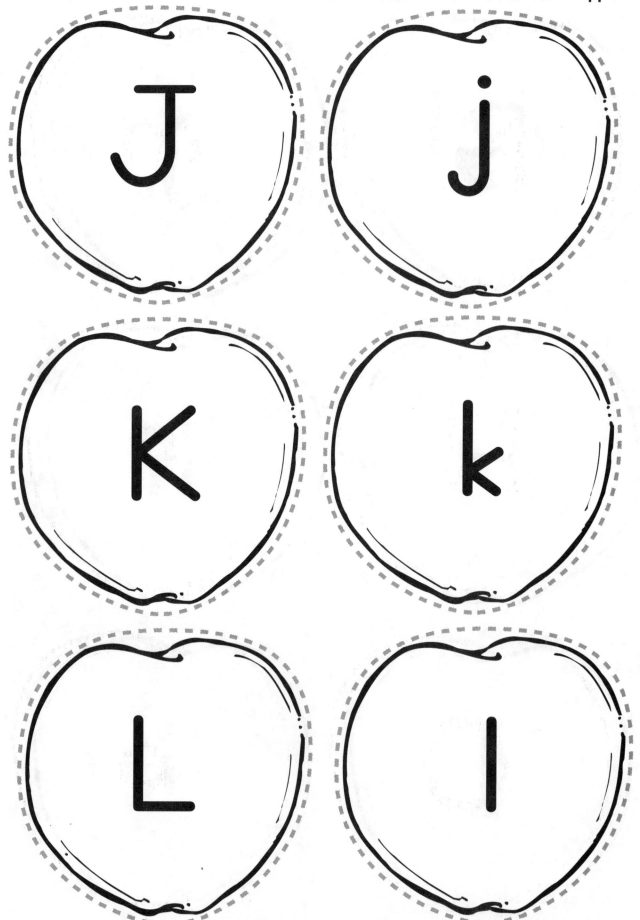

Note: Reproduce the apple forms to use with the game on page 84.

Patterns for Apple Match

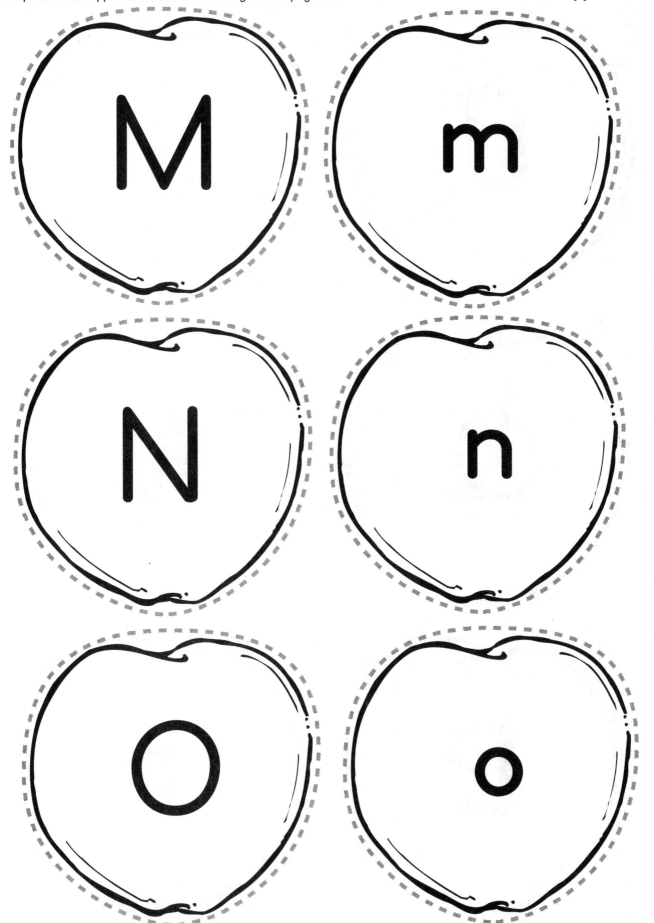

Note: Reproduce the apple forms to use with the game on page 84.

Patterns for Apple Match

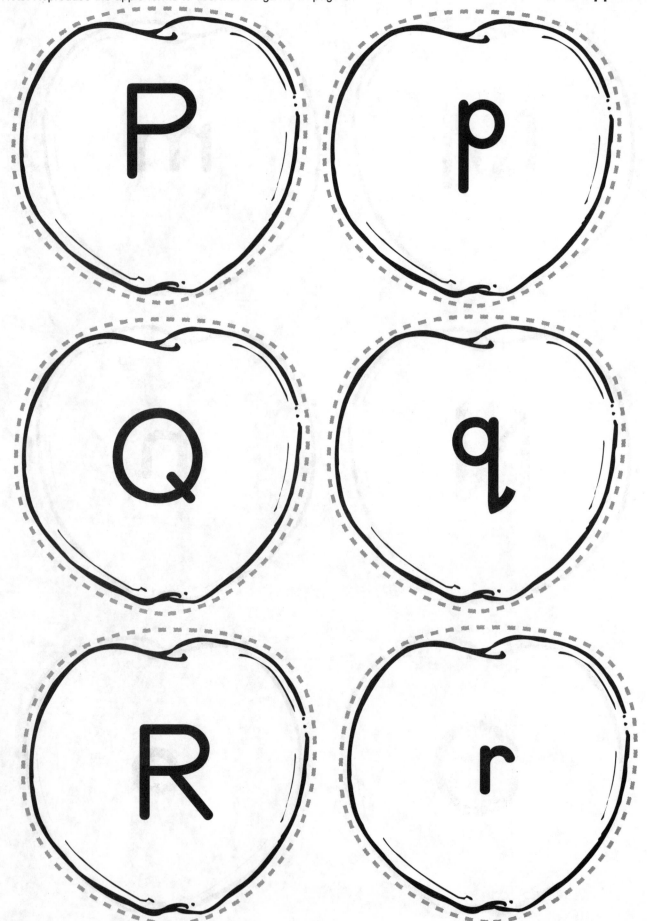

Note: Reproduce the apple forms to use with the game on page 84.

Patterns for Apple Match

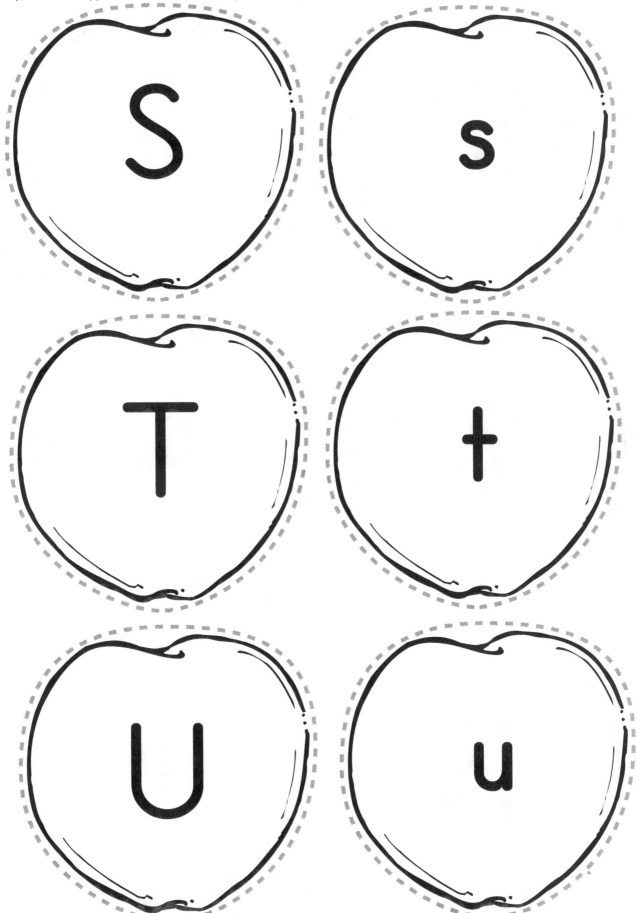

Note: Reproduce the apple forms to use with the game on page 84.

Patterns for Apple Match

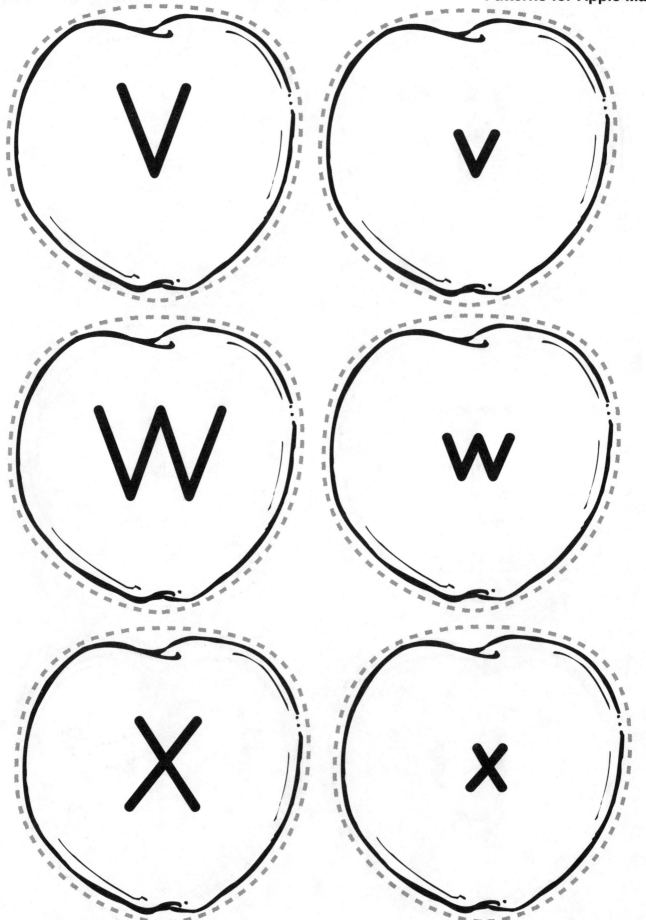

Note: Reproduce the apple forms to use with the game on page 84. Reproduce the "wormy apples" to use with the letter identification game on page 86.

Patterns for Apple Match

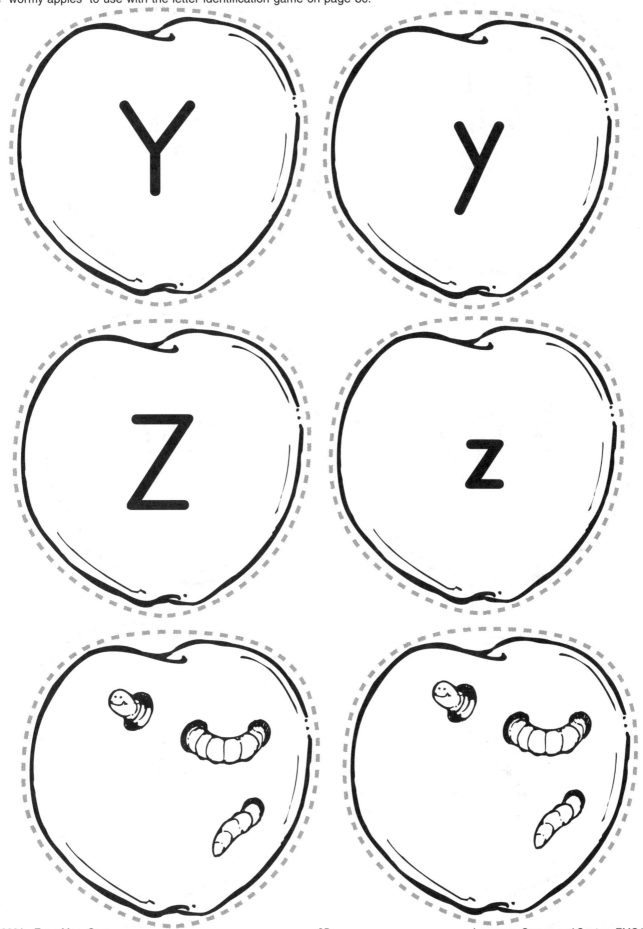

95

What's in My Bag?

How to Make

1. You will need one lunch-sized paper bag and one small object (items commonly found around the classroom —scissors, crayons, toy, apple, etc.) per player.

2. Put one item in each bag and fold the top closed.

96

How to Play

1. Students sit in a line facing the teacher. The teacher has the bags.

   This game is not as easy for students as it sounds. The teacher should model the activity one or more times.

2. A student picks a bag and stands by the teacher. He/She peeks inside the bag and then gives a description of the object, ending by asking "What's in my bag?"

   Be prepared to prompt the student doing the describing. Ask questions such as:

What color is it?	Can you eat it?
What is it used for?	What shape is it?
What is it made of?	How big is it?

3. The other students try to guess what is in the bag. If they cannot guess the item, the student with the bag gives another clue.

4. The game ends when each student has had a turn.

It is red.
You can eat it.

Playing with Beginners

Play the game as a guessing game with the teacher doing the describing. Students listen carefully and raise their hand when they think they know what is in the bag. Explain each step of the description so students get the idea of what a description is. For example, if you put a pencil in the bag you might say:

- I'm going to tell you its color—it is yellow.
- I'm going to tell you its shape—it is long and thin.
- I'm going to tell what it is made of—it is made of wood and graphite.
- I'm going to tell you what it is used for—it is used to write.

After students have guessed it, review your description as you show the object.

Advanced Play for Beginning Readers

Write a letter on the outside of each bag and put in an item that begins with that letter (a—apple, b—book, etc.). Play the game as usual, reminding students that the object begins with the sound made by the letter printed on the bag.

It is yellow. It is long and thin. It is made of wood and graphite.

The Three Bears

How to Make

1. Reproduce the bears, chairs, beds, and bowls on pages 101 - 104. You will need all three sizes of the same object for each student playing the game.

2. Color, laminate, and cut out the objects.

How to Play The Three Bears

1. Have students sit in a circle with the teacher. Give each student a set of three objects. Alternate sets so that each player has a different set than the player on either side.

2. Ask students to lay out their pictures from the largest to the smallest. Ask each student to point to the largest and smallest and tell about them. ("This bowl is the largest. This bowl is the smallest.")

3. After all children have told about their pictures, have them mix up their pictures and pass them to the person sitting next to them. Repeat step two.

4. Teacher collects the pieces by asking students to hand her their largest piece. Ask "Now what piece is larger?" Collect those pieces. Finally collect the smallest pieces.

Play with Beginners

Teacher puts out one picture and describes it. (For example: Put out Papa Bear. Say "Papa Bear is the biggest.") Have each student put out their largest picture and describe it. Repeat with the smallest pictures.

This bed is the biggest.

Patterns for The Three Bears

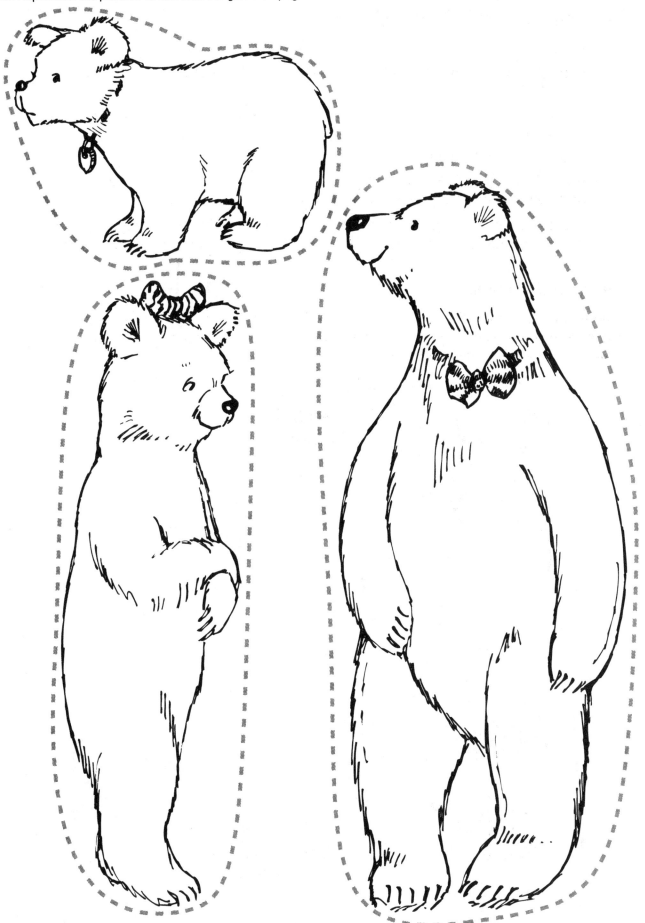

 Language Games and Centers EMC 736

Note: Reproduce the pictures to use with the game on page 99.

Patterns for The Three Bears

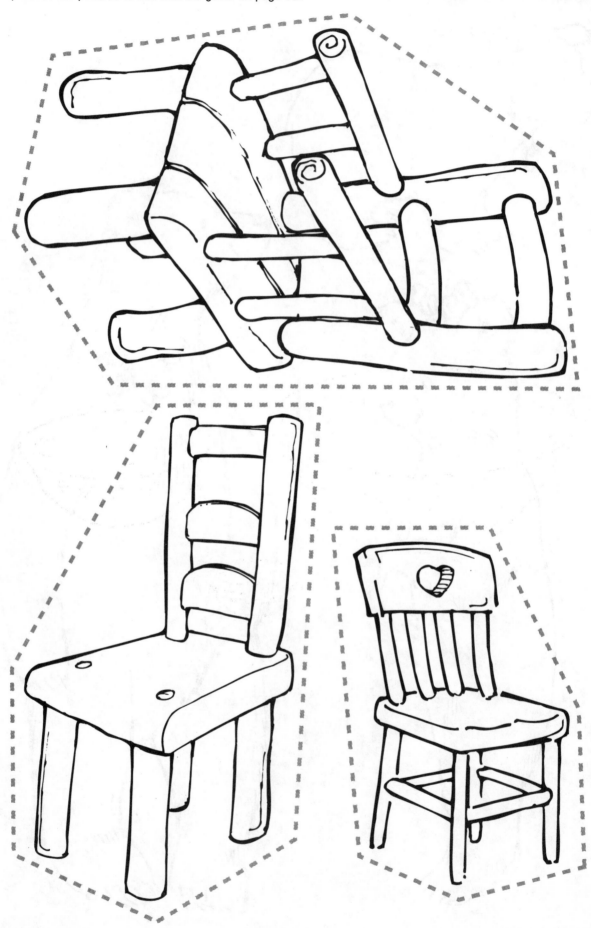

Note: Reproduce the pictures to use with the game on page 99.

Patterns for The Three Bears

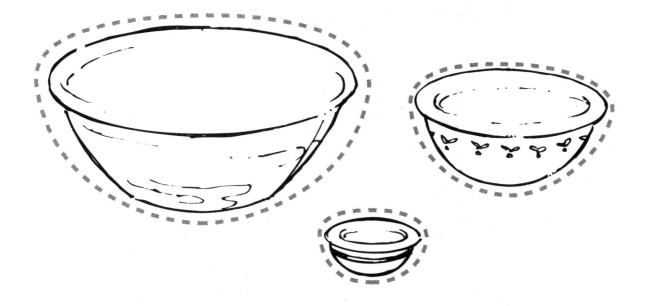

Note: Reproduce the pictures to use with the game on page 99.

Patterns for The Three Bears

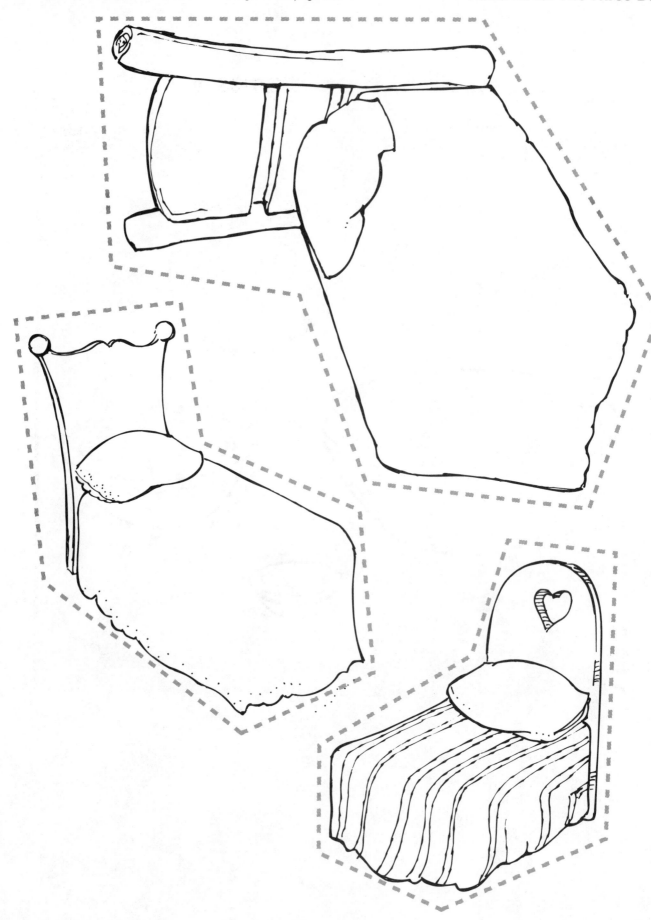

Pizza Time Rhymes

(up to six players)

How to Make

1. Reproduce the pizza pies on pages 107 - 109.

2. Reproduce the pizza slices on pages 110 - 112.

3. Color, laminate, and cut out the pizza pies and slices.

How to Play

1. Students sit in a line facing the teacher. Number of players is limited to six.

2. Pass out a pizza pie to each student. Be sure the student can name the picture on the pie. Teacher keeps the pizza slices. (If not all pies are used, make sure the slices correspond to those pies.)

3. The teacher explains that students are to fill their pizza pie with words that rhyme. Teacher then holds up a pizza slice, names the picture, and asks "Who needs this piece of pizza?" The student that claims the piece tells why it is his/hers ("I need cat. It rhymes with hat."

4. If no one claims the slice, the teacher holds it by each pizza and has each student say both picture names to see if it rhymes with their pizza ("cat-hug, cat-spoon, cat-hat").

5. Play continues until all pizzas are covered.

Play with Beginners

A great deal of oral rhyming practice is needed before children can be successful playing rhyming games.

Lay the pizza pies in a row in front of the students. (Begin with two pies and work up to all six.) Teacher holds a slice of pizza by a pie and says both picture names. The group decides if the words rhyme.

Advanced Play for More Skillful Players

As the students become more familiar with rhyming words they can be asked to name more words that rhyme with their card match. For example, if the pizza pie says sock, the student with the rhyming slice might say "block, rock, tock, Spock, flock," etc.) Other players might also add to the list.

Note: Reproduce the patterns to use with the game on page 105.

Patterns for Pizza Time Rhymes

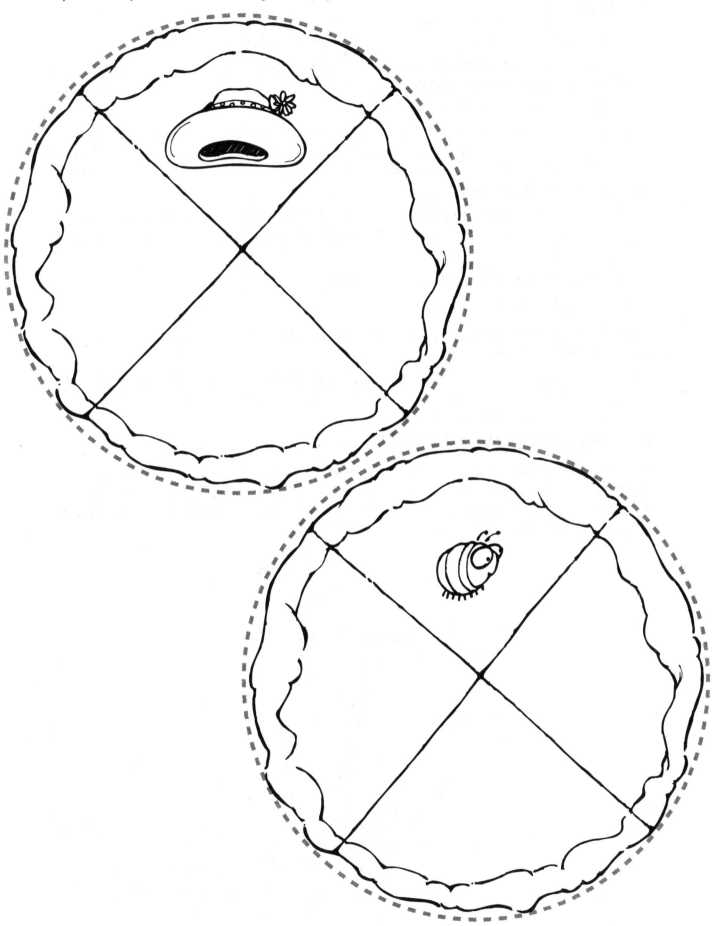

Patterns for Pizza Time Rhymes

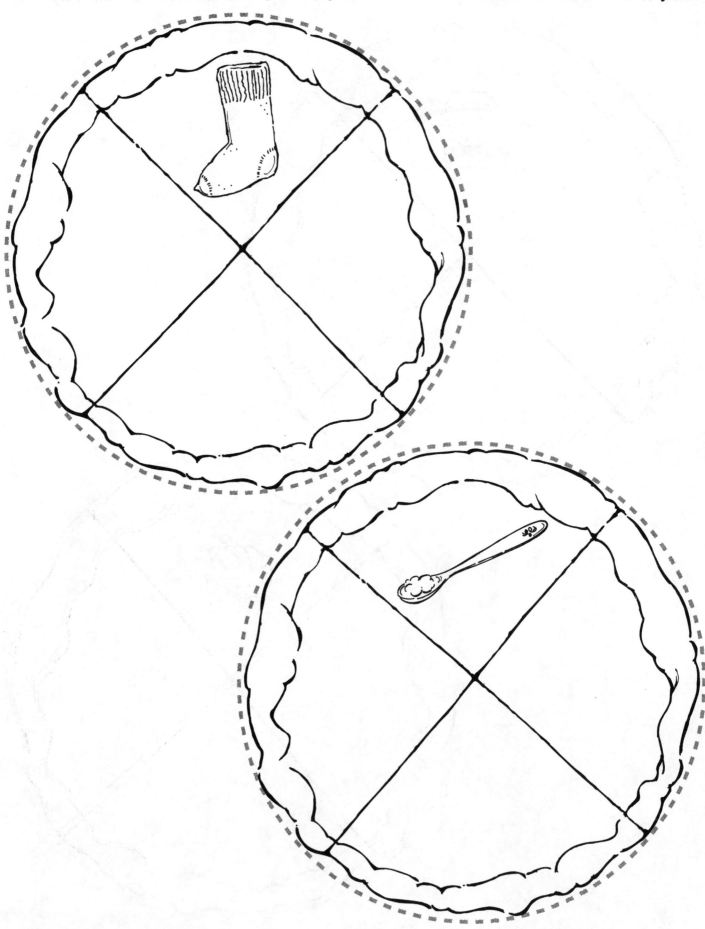

Note: Reproduce the patterns to use with the game on page 105.

Patterns for Pizza Time Rhymes

Patterns for Pizza Time Rhymes

Note: Reproduce the pictures to use with the game on page 105.

Patterns for Pizza Time Rhymes

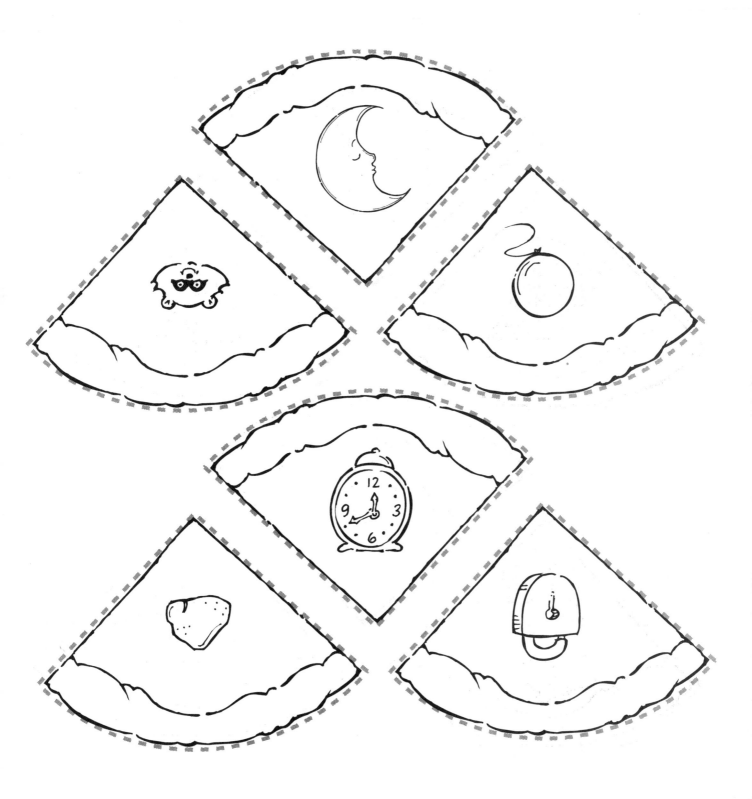

Note: Reproduce the pictures to use with the game on page 105.

Patterns for Pizza Time Rhymes